PRIVATE PAIN

A Pastor's Struggle through Katrina

Dr. DeBruce Nelson

Private Pain — A Pastor's Struggle through Katrina
Copyright ©2007 Dr. DeBruce Nelson
& Words2Empower Publishers

All rights reserved. The copyright law of the United States of America protects this book.

Published by: Words2Empower Publishers

1st Printing, 2007

No part of this book may be reproduced or transmitted in any form or by any means, electronic or mechanical, including photocopying, recording, or by any information storage and retrieval system, without permission in writing from the publisher. The publication is designed to provide accurate and authoritative information in regard to the subject matter covered.

Books are available at special discounts for bulk purchases, sales promotion, fundraising, or educational purposes.

Cover Design: Solomon Edmond

Book Design: Yvonne Vermillion

Project Director: Duane Harvey

ISBN: # 978-0-9790213-4-3

For more information, write to:
Bishop DeBruce Nelson Ministries
Lighthouse Apostolic Holiness Church
769 Division St
Biloxi, MS 39530
Jgn719@centurytel.net

OR

Words2Empower Publishers
P.O. Box 4964
Capitol Heights, Maryland, 20791   USA
www.wpublishers.com
1-888-925-BOOK (2665)
For Worldwide Distribution
Printed in Canada

PRIVATE PAIN
A Pastor's Struggle through Katrina

"This book shows a refreshing honesty that was not relayed by the scores of pictures displayed by Katrina. It takes you deep inside the inner being of a man of faith — a man who was forced to practice what he preached, and in fact found out that what he preached wasn't personally real until he practiced it."

– Dr. R. A. Powell Jr., Acclaimed author of *Pattern of Purpose*, Motivational Speaker, and Pastor of Monument of Joy Ministries.

"Bishop Nelson has a unique and appealing way of telling a story that makes his books quite unique, and this huge best seller is no exception. Here he sets the stage for his brilliant trilogy on pain by chronicling the events surrounding the most catastrophic hurricane, Katrina. Its total cost in terms of human life and unnecessary destruction is a cautionary lesson for history."

– Rev. Ronnie Nsubuga, bestselling author of *A Legacy of Choices*.

DEDICATION

To one of the world's greatest heroes who has impacted my life, Bishop Leroy Floyd Nelson, my father, deceased, for his loyal friendship and faithfulness to his family's birth, spiritual and natural, and foremost to the Gospel of Jesus Christ. Bishop Nelson was a father who poured strength, honor, and integrity into his sons. He left a legacy of which his eldest son, Apostle Floyd E. Nelson, is the overseer. Bishop Nelson was an ideal model of both disciple and disciple-maker, having dedicated himself to fulfilling 2Timothy 4:7, *"I have fought the good fight, I have finished my course, and I have kept the faith."*

Table of Contents

ACKNOWLEDGEMENT 1

FOREWORD 3

PREFACE
    Understanding Storms 5

INTRODUCTION
    A Story of Katrina Disaster Made Public 7

Chapter One
CONFRONTING THE PAIN OF THE PAST 11
    The Day before Hurricane Katrina 11
    The Longest Day 13
    Helping People in Crisis: 17
    Encountering Loss 19

Chapter Two
COPING WITH TRAGEDY 29
    Seven Years of Toiling, Over Within Twelve Hours 30
    Here We Go Again. 32
    Depleted Community 37
    A Chance To Make A Difference 42
    The Drive To Overcome 45

Chapter Three
THE POWER OF PAIN 53
    The Purpose of Pain 54
    Deluge, Death, and Debris 57
    Solving Problems 60
    Teamwork 62
    The Theology of Suffering 63
    Turning Pain into Purpose 66

Chapter Four
STRUGGLING TO SURVIVE 71
   Hope in a Hopeless Situation 76
   Tragicomedy 82
   Strategic Alliances 83
   Pain Unspeakable 87
   The Comeback 88

Chapter Five
TREASURE IN THE TRAGEDY 93
   Being A Blessing When I Needed A Blessing 95

Chapter Six
I THINK, THEREFORE I AM 99

Chapter Seven
MIRACLE OR TRAGEDY, WE PRAISE GOD 105
   Praising God No Matter Your Condition 107
   Hindrances to Praise 110
   Hearts of Gratitude 111

Chapter Eight
DISASTER RECOVERY PROCESS 113
   One Month after Katrina 114
   Building Back 117
   Six Months After: From Private Pain To Public Praise ... 119
   Rebuilding 120
   The Devil's PR Department 122
   Christ's PR Department 123
   Positive Outlook 123

Chapter Nine
TWO YEARS AFTER KATRINA 125
   A Cry of Help 125

ABOUT THE AUTHOR 129

ACKNOWLEDGEMENT

This book is in no small measure dedicated to the faithful support and encouragement of Rev. Ronnie Nsubuga and the rest of the staff of Words2Empower Publishers. I have enjoyed a close and fruitful relationship over the months with Ronnie who has made this dream a reality. I am grateful to The Lord for the ministry of Dr. R. A. Powell, Jr., who encouraged me to write this book.

Also, I am particularly grateful to Duane Harvey for his inimitable skill, Solomon Edmond for the Cover Design, Chuck and Yvonne at Helppublish.com and Magicgraphix.com for the editing and layout, and also the entire staff of Words2empower Publishers who worked hard under very pressing deadlines to keep this book on schedule throughout the editorial and typesetting process. Their kindness, patience, and diligence have been exemplary, even under difficult circumstances.

My special thanks to my lovely and supportive wife who has the epitome of Job's patience with this work and with me, and to all those in my church congregation who have also been prayerful and supportive.

Dr. DeBruce Nelson

FOREWORD

Dr. Wanda A. Davis-Turner; author, minister, counselor

While I admit that there is not one living person on Earth (shepherd, sheep, leader, pastor, prophet, layperson, adult, child, male or female) who has not experienced failure, pain, loss, catastrophic or shocking circumstances, I must declare that some of us seem to experience great losses, pain, shock, failure, and catastrophic situations more often than others. Such is the case with Dr. DeBruce Nelson in his new book *PRIVATE PAIN, A Pastor's Struggle with Katrina*!

Never have I read a more compelling and truthful account of one of this nation's disastrous, ruinous events — Katrina! Dr. Nelson, somehow, is able to gather every thought, emotion, and action he experienced while walking through the tragic events leading up to the storm, while walking through the storm, and while now living victoriously in the aftermath of the storm. Even as he shared compelling page after compelling page, I saw splinters of my own life's experiences; you know, those that rocked your boat, those that crippled you for more than a moment, and those historical events that re-framed your life forever, or so it seems. And, somehow, the things of my past became diminished as I realized that somewhere, someone today is going through something far greater than I could ever imagine. Worse, someone is still dealing with the residue of a past experience, and their residue may be more horrendous than any full-life happening I may have seen, heard about, or lived through. They, like Dr. Nelson, may realize: "Katrina *ain't over yet*"!

If you are looking for an easy read — put this book down! If you want to be challenged, *spirit, soul, and body*, to grow up, to develop and to mature into the person God birthed you to become

Dr. DeBruce Nelson

in your *genesis*, then this book, this manual for life, is for you! Don't be shocked or amazed to find out that there is at least one other believer on planet Earth who feels what you feel, thinks what you think, and who wants what you want! That person is Dr. DeBruce Nelson. One of his most compelling discussions pertains to a quote from John F. Kennedy, "We would like to live as we once lived, but history will not permit it." From this, Dr. Nelson discusses *"Sankofa"* – *while* sharing that it is an Akan (Ghanaiam) word which means 'One must return to the past in order to move forward.' *"Sankofa"* is a mythic bird that flies forward while looking backward with an egg in its mouth (symbolizing the future). This mythic bird visually and symbolically allows us the opportunity to consider how, together, we should reach back and gather the best of what our past has to teach us so that we can achieve our full potential as we move forward. With everything in his life having been lost, damaged, or destroyed, it seemed, Dr. Nelson was able to find a way to perpetually minister and teach others what to do when their "storm hits". What a slap to Satan's face, that when down, ourselves, we still find a way to lift others up.

Dr. Nelson, you remind us again and again that: *Whatever we have lost, forgotten, forgiven, or have been stripped of can be reclaimed, revived, preserved, and perpetuated!... We know that we can't change what has happened yesterday. But we can learn from yesterday's mistakes, and with God's Help we can use that knowledge to make a better tomorrow,* (Chapter One, Page 9). Will it be easy? You didn't promise us that, and neither did The Lord! Will it be impossible? No, for with Christ, nothing is impossible! Will we turn things around immediately? Of course not, because, "To everything there is a season and a time to every purpose." Your book, Dr. Nelson, is a powerful tool to help people all over the world to make sense of "Katrina" and then begin navigating through the storms of their own lives, to bring closure, renewal, and revival for a better and brighter tomorrow!

PREFACE

Understanding Storms

Storms are things which threaten our well-being. Storms can be either literal or figurative. Literal storms may include tornadoes, hurricanes, or floods which may take away all we own, and, perhaps, even our loved ones. How we respond to such tragedies will reveal the quality of our worth. Will we be emotionally devastated? Or will we be able to stand strong and be willing to continue without despair? Figurative storms may involve illness, loss of loved ones, financial setbacks, all which may take away our health, family, or possessions. How we respond to such tragedies will reveal the quality of our true identity.

Often, God brings us storms in order to speak to us; storms get our attention. In our lives, we use idiomatic phrases in a variety of situations which enable us to communicate enormous amounts of information in an economical way. In a sort of leverage of language, phrases such as, "Hang in there," and, "Lighten up," or, "Go for it," connote meaning far beyond the few words expressed. The scriptures also contain such phrases — for example, "Endure to the end," and, "Verily, verily, I say unto you," or, "It came to pass." One phrase, however, which seems to be particularly useful to The Lord and from which we might gain some insight into The Lord's personality is the frequently used counsel, "Be of good cheer." The scriptures record The Lord speaking these words in a wide variety of situations to encourage, to comfort, to lift, to inspire, to convey compassion, to build hope, to validate faith, and to teach perspective. It lifts my spirit to imagine those various situations.

At the same time, after the disciples participated with Jesus in the miraculous feeding of more than five thousand, Jesus asked his disciples to get into a ship and to go before him to the west side of the Sea of Galilee. Left to their own strength against the contrary winds, they toiled against the sea for several hours while attempting to cover the few miles to their destination. Exhausted from the struggle at their oars, they were also certainly deeply discouraged and frightened as the ship stalled against the waves in the midst of the sea. Jesus came unto them while they were doing what he asked and walked on the water as he approached the troubled ship. Sensing their fear, Jesus calmed them by saying, *"Be of good cheer; it is I; be not afraid."* (Matthew 14:27)

Tragic events come into our lives regardless of who we are, and they sometimes strike so suddenly. Christ has said, *"Peace I leave with you, my peace I give unto you. ... Let not your heart be troubled, neither let it be afraid."* (John 14:27)

INTRODUCTION

A Story of Katrina Disaster Made Public

In over 154 years of storm tracking, Hurricane Katrina has been labeled as the costliest, busiest, and one of the deadliest hurricanes in the history of the United States. The cost from her damage has exceeded $81.2 billion, and fatalities, directly and indirectly, have topped at least 1,836 lives with an additional 705 people still reported missing.

The shock and awe I experienced during and after Hurricane Katrina is beyond my power to fully describe. Even as I do so now, I feel a prickly sensation crawling across my shoulders and moving up and down my spine. At this, I close my eyes and shake my head, while saying, "Mmmph... have mercy."

Why have mercy? Because as Katrina slowly slips out of the national consciousness, I wake up to her everyday. Sometimes I go to sleep with her, and on occasion she wakes me up at night. Sometimes she vexes my spirit so unmercifully that instead of fighting back, I have to just be *still*. Just be *still* and let God deal with her.

People think that as a Pastor and a self-proclaimed man of God that I am constantly plugged into the Higher Power. Well, I am human just like anyone else. I don't change clothes in a phone booth and become superhuman. I'm just a person who knows that I wouldn't be where I am if it weren't for the Grace of God. What makes God sovereign is that He is God, and I am not!

> **As Katrina slowly slips out of national consciousness, I wake up to her everyday.**

Dr. DeBruce Nelson

At first, I wasn't sure I even wanted to revisit those early days of Katrina and run the risk of reopening some of those still-healing wounds. I say this because although some of the imagery is sketchy, the emotional pain has perfect recall. For that reason, this book is not an attempt to sell God cheap, but to show how He can keep someone amidst private pain while in a public place.

For instance, when I think about two of my female church members who weathered the storm alone in their apartments, that alone gives me pause. First, I will share about Theresa: When the waters started to rise and come into her apartment's lower floor, her heart began to pound loudly in her chest. She had no way of crying out to anyone except The Lord. Her parents, children, and friends had evacuated the city. She looked around her apartment and began to assess all she had worked for, and she thought those things were replaceable. By now her car was under water, but that was replaceable. However, to save herself from drowning, she vowed to survive for her grandchildren and the rest of the family. She knew that she had to come up with a plan for survival.

She narrates that divine instruction came to her, telling her to count her steps to the upstairs space. God was getting ready to work a miracle right before her eyes. She did as she was instructed, and a still, small voice whispered to her to go and lie down and take a nap. The waters were at the eleventh step, which had one more step before reaching the upper lever. Before lying on the bed, she looked down from her window, and she could see that the rushing water below was carrying cars, overturning cars, and literally ripping roofs from apartments. Then, all of a sudden, a deep weariness came over her right before she slept. She didn't know exactly how long she slept, but when she awakened, she got up from the bed and went to the stairs landing to assess the water level. Remembering that before going to sleep there had been eleven steps underwater, she thought she had miscounted or forgotten. Immediately, she began to count the steps again:

PRIVATE PAIN

ONE, TWO, THREE, and so on. She counted down to eight or nine steps and began to rejoice. She knew right then that the water was receding. She had a praise going on right there in her wet apartment. She praised God for leading her and for delivering her from the angry waters that wanted so much to claim her, as it was doing to so many others.

Another amazing story was of a mother and daughter who weathered the storm. Their only advantage was that their house was of a higher survival advantage over Theresa's because it had a double attic. High surges were coming from the beach area as well as Back Bay, so they were confronted by a double battle. Nita and her daughter's downstairs space had filled with water quickly. It was a blessing that they had The Lord to guide them through survival skills. As they looked through their upper windows, they saw the dark waters of Back Bay meet with the clearer waters of the beach, and this battle lasted for over eight hours. This mother and daughter determined to cling to each other for life. They knew that if they had to die, they would die together, as they watched the combative waters attempt to claim their home as one of its victims.

Whatever the reason for your discontent, Katrina definitely was mine. To me, Katrina is no longer a storm or even a metaphor, she is carved in stone — a defining historical moment. She is a line in the sand, a hallmark. She is like World War I and II. She is the 9/11. In view of this, I am like a split-screen television. The person I was before Katrina — I keep looking for him in the same way I keep looking for missing items in my house which I believe I am still somehow, someway, and somewhere going to find.

Before Katrina, I didn't think about the pain and the pleasure-principles — the ones which say that we seek to maximize our pleasure and minimize our pain. I thought it was merely psycho-babble. In that way, I was very much like the old Sam Cooke song,

"Don't Know Much about History." Today, I know something about it. I know what it is like to have your whole body riddled with an anxiety which feels like 1,000 pricks of a needle all at once.

I know what it is like to have a dark night of the soul when you can't eat, you can't sleep, and all you want is a rest from your other self. I know what it is like when the chambers of your soul is filled with melancholy and dread to the point that you close yourself off to the Holy Spirit. And what makes matters worse comes with knowing that despite how you feel, others are depending on you. What makes this feeling particularly dark is the sheer reality of knowing that you cannot afford the rent anymore to stay in your current residence. And not only are you being evicted, but you are forced by court order to watch your stuff being put out on the curb. You are forced to watch your prized couch being thrown down with no respect, knowing that you had the hardest time getting it inside the residence in the first place. You are forced to watch your big-screen TV brought out, knowing that not only do you have no place to put it, but you also know that it contributed to your not being able to pay your rent.

I know what it's like when your heart pounds so much that you just want to rip it out. I know what it is to feel as though someone is shaking a rattle in your stomach. I know of many people who have suffered far greater hardships who still continue, but it doesn't take away the private pain, even if it does give you a flicker of light. Nevertheless, no matter who I thought I was before Katrina, I now realize that we live in a small world. Just to think, earlier on television I had seen a Tsunami in Indonesia, and although my heart went out to those people, I couldn't really connect with their pain until Katrina made the connection for me.

Most people are hesitant to discuss pain, but in this book I encourage individuals to do so, because if you don't open up — you blow up.

Chapter One
CONFRONTING THE PAIN OF THE PAST

*S*ankofa is an Akan (Ghanaian) word which means, "One must return to the past in order to move forward." Visually and symbolically, *Sankofa* is expressed as a mythic bird that flies forward while looking backward with an egg (symbolizing the future) in its mouth. Sankofa allows us the opportunity to consider how, together, we should reach back and gather the best of what our past has to teach us so that we can achieve our full potential as we move forward. Whatever we have lost, forgotten, forgone, or have been stripped of, can be reclaimed, revived, preserved, and perpetuated. We all have some regrets about the past and try to forget our mistakes. We know that we can't change what happened yesterday. But we *can* learn from yesterday's mistakes, and with God's Help we can use that knowledge to make a better tomorrow.

The Day before Hurricane Katrina

I was serving as the Pastor of Lighthouse Church in Biloxi (Bi-LUX-e), Mississippi, the day before Katrina struck, and we finished church around 12:30 P.M. My sermon that day was "Unknown God Reveals Himself to Mankind." After locking up the church, I looked up at the sky, and although it was cloudy, there was no strong indication that Katrina was going to be what she became. The media anticipation was stating that this could be the "Big One", as they

> We all have some regrets about the past and try to forget our mistakes.

Dr. DeBruce Nelson

were now saying it was a Category 5 and was expected to hit the Gulf Coast within 24 hours. Because of that, I said a prayer of protection for the saints who were still there and for those who had left town beforehand. A lot of people had evacuated that morning anticipating huge traffic build-ups on the major highways, such as: Interstate 10 and 90 — both of which led out of Biloxi. Naturally we hugged each other, promising to stay in phone contact. A part of me wished that I could have taken the people determined to tough it out with me, because by living 45 minutes away in Alabama, we were reported to have not been hit as hard as those in the Mississippi Gulfport Region of Biloxi, Gulfport, the Pass, and the Bay.

The fact is, despite the ever-darkening skies and slight wind gusts, on the drive back home, my wife and I wondered if Katrina was going to match the media hype. Just in case, we decided to take precautions against the storm, because even though the media can distort one's mind by blowing things out of proportion or by focusing on the negative, we didn't want to live with any after-the-fact regrets. So we boarded up the windows with plywood and prepared for whatever would happen, and being a "faith in God" person, there was no need to cross my fingers.

That night we knew how important it was to get some sleep, because if the storm did come, then who knew when one could possibly sleep? That night we prayed for the saints, and I tried my best to relax.

When the first bands of light wind and light rain began coming in overnight, there was no indication that this was going to be, as the National Weather Service was suggesting, "an Apocalyptic Hurricane". Being a Preacher, I knew a good metaphor when I heard one, but I also knew how people use language as a sphere of influence. After all, there was only moderate force to the wind, but it was still nothing to sneeze at. Yet when the lightning started coming, I began to rethink of the biblical storm.

The Longest Day

In 1959, Cornelius Ryan, an Irish journalist and author mainly known for his writings on popular military history, wrote a well-known book, *The Longest Day*, which tells the story of the D-Day invasion of Normandy on June 6, 1944. "D-Day" often represents a variable which designates the day upon which some significant event will occur or has occurred. In life, there always comes a specific day when an all-out attack is launched against you. Everything you are going through is training you for one specific day, and today *could* be that day. Everything you went through in your life was preparing you for this divine moment. God wanted to see if you remembered everything He put within you. Every day is not the same; the enemy is looking for the right day when you are at your weakest point and don't feel like praying. That is the day when he wants to launch an attack. Paul the Apostle talks of an "evil day", *"put on the full armor of God so when the day of evil comes..."* (Ephesians 6:13)

The day of hurricane Katrina was indeed my longest day. That morning my wife and I got up around 5:00 A.M., and we were still thankful that everything was fully intact. The wind had picked up to around 15 mph, but it was still manageable.

Before long, the phone calls started coming in. People were starting to become concerned.

I tried my best to reassure them, reminding them that God was watching over us. No sooner than I hung up with one call than another one came in. Sometimes a call came on the landline and other times on the cellphone. There was a rising tension in these phone calls, and I could tell that people were genuinely concerned. Yet, I had no frame of reference for this unspoken tension. I was tempted to say people were overreacting, but I knew way better than that. It was getting tough to mediate, because as soon as I would get a mental picture, someone else would reframe my picture. Some of them still had electric power — others did not. The wind was shattering windows and doing punching combinations to some people's property, and others viewed it simply as a super-hard rain. Either way, since we weren't experiencing the same intensity, I began to wish that I could trade places with some of them, especially some of those precious church mothers.

Still, I felt like a pharmacist dispensing spiritual medication, reminding this person of God's unfailing Goodness, and reminding another person that He promised to never leave us nor ever forsake us.

I'm not saying that my power to Pastor was rendered ineffective, but it seemed slightly odd, because despite my heavenly words of comfort, people were clearly looking at the hell they were seeing.

I made a mental note to find out what this condition is besides being scared or fearful. One doesn't have to be Tom Cruise to have suspicions of psychology, but information can be empowering. (I later on found out that this situation is called 'Cognitive Dissonance' — that state of tension when you recognize the inconsistencies in your thoughts, feelings, and opinions, or in short, inconsistencies between what you know or believe and what the new information is telling you.)

I began to wonder, *What could they be going through that those of us who had experienced Camille could not withstand?* You see, for those of us on or near the Gulf Coast, our shared history of growing up in a hurricane culture helps and hinders in times like these. Part of the reason is because Camille, a Category 5 Hurricane of 1969, was the benchmark or stumbling block for all of us. As the collective reasoning went, "If we made it through

PRIVATE PAIN

Camille, and if her storm surge hadn't gotten that far, and her winds were bearable, we can make it through Katrina."

Besides the fact that Camille ended up killing 143 when she struck the Golf Coast, she did only minor structural damage — 2 to 6 inches in most cases, and up to 10 inches in the extreme. She was the rule of thumb that had most of us joking, "Ain't no way, baby girl, that Katrina could do more damage."

In a region threatened by so-called violent storms, it seems to me now that we grew a little complacent between each storm. If the predicted storm didn't match the hype, then we tended to wave it off. On top of developing alligator-type skin, some of us got a little dismissive of anything less than a category 3 hurricane.

As daylight came, the calls steadily came in, with some calling back again for good measure. By in large, the vast majority were saying that they were peeping out of their windows and that they were seeing all kind of debris flying around. Some people reported that the wind was sweeping water from side to side like a mop. In some cases trees were being uprooted, cars were being lifted, and objects were being thrown like knives. Some even likened it to a steam bath because of the ever-present mist. Some reported high, smacking winds which they estimated to be around 120 mph, while some simply said it was ferocious.

Knowing how those wind-driven waves can be, I was concerned mostly for those who lived within blocks of the Gulf of Mexico and Back Bay.

I knew that hurricanes could spawn a tornado or two, but from what everyone was saying, this was a regular hurricane. We looked out the windows, and although it was blowing, it still wasn't on the same level as the wind in Biloxi. Small as it is, Biloxi, a 300-year-old fishing town turned casino magnet and with a population of around 50,000, couldn't withstand the storm that people were reporting. According to them, the wind was raging from all sides and from all directions, on top of pelting them with vicious rain. Even with that, all of us know that it is the storm surge which makes the situation deadly. So far, I hadn't heard anything about a storm surge. And the fact that some people still had power was a good sign — I thought.

When we looked at the news on TV, they were mainly showing New Orleans, but they did give an indication that the storm had turned east and that Mississippi was in for the worst of it. We prayed for all involved, hoping that all would be spared.

By 8:00 A.M., the calls were steadily coming in. By my church member's collective tone of voice, I could tell that something was going horribly wrong. It started to dawn on me that perhaps we had miscalculated this storm. Had we thought this through? Had this been predictable? Part of the answer to that question lies in the fact that we are always trying to measure something, trying to put something under a microscope, and trying to find a way to box everything into categories.

From the Biloxi perspective, it was clear that Katrina didn't want to be defined like that. Ohhh, she didn't mind if people talked about her after she made her presence felt, but it would be after the fact.

The phone calls kept coming. Some were reporting houses falling like cards. Katrina was ripping off roofs, snapping trees like toothpicks, spinning cars like a basketball on your fingertip, then slamming them down like a two-year-old kid with toys. Houses were being ripped apart like paper, and Katrina was putting Biloxi through a shredding machine. A chill ran down my spine; it was a distress signal, I suppose — the first of many which Katrina would deposit into my system. Immediately, pressure filled my head like a sinus headache.

PRIVATE PAIN

Helping People in Crisis:

"We would like to live as we once lived, but history will not permit it," said John F. Kennedy. Those words have never rung more true for Americans since Sept. 11, 2001. Americans are dealing with a new and sometimes frightening reality.

> "We would like to live as we once lived, but history will not permit it," said John F. Kennedy.

Coping with a tragedy is not always easy. Crisis hits all people at some time in their lives. When crisis strikes, people need help. According to Richard E. Dodge, a Young Adults' Sunday School Teacher in Nashville, TN, "Before jumping into the middle of a crisis, make sure you are prepared. Some well-meaning efforts have created more harm than good when the people responding create confusion or fail to say or do the right thing." He further offers some tips on how to respond effectively during a crisis, "Be a good listener, and have a loving and accepting attitude. Attempt to help in practical ways, and ask what specific things you can do to help."

It's natural to feel more or less inadequate when a friend or relative tells you his or her troubles. Actually, you may be able to help — perhaps far more than you think. You may not be able to solve another person's problems, but neighbors, friends, and relatives who show warmth and have common sense can provide important support.

It's natural to feel inadequate when someone — perhaps a friend or relative — tells you their troubles, but you can often be of real assistance. Burdens which are shared with a friend are often lighter to carry. Discussing your troubles with someone is a way of expressing emotions and can help get rid of some of the effects.

Dr. DeBruce Nelson

I began to have this inner dialogue with myself, *Should I give the people what they want?... No, just give them what they need.* I thought, *You can't just give them anything you feel like. Be careful of what you say . . . Be careful what you tell them to do or not to do.* A part of me began to panic and pace because I couldn't see the right thing to do. My wife reassured me that I was doing the right thing by simply being there for the people, but it didn't feel that way. I nodded in agreement, thankful that we were at least striving in this together.

When the phone calls kept coming in and confirming the viciousness of the storm, I started to feel more defeat than sadness. I know I am just one person, but there had to be something I could do. It wasn't like I was mad at God, but it appeared as if He had lifted His Hands and was letting this go on. I had to get over that mindset, knowing that if you destroy the root, you cannot grow back the limb. However, my heart couldn't help but go out to people. I thought about the six senior citizens who had decided to be there for each other and how they had just reported to me that water was coming every twenty minutes, one foot at a time.

To be painstakingly honest, I felt like a marionette — one of those puppets that hangs by its strings — except that I had several broken strings. I wanted to know my part in all of this. It was all starting to be a mystery to me. The real significance seemed beyond my grasp. This is usually the part when people start screaming, but I had my wife to consider. Some things are hard to comprehend, because some things I can barely understand myself. All I know is that I struggled with the practical applications of my spirituality.

In the midst of talking to people, I began to pray inside of myself for God to cover me and spread His precious Love all over me, hiding me in Him before I lose my mind. I say this because, sometimes, like an actor on a stage or a ballplayer, all you can do is own the moment and trust your instinctive feelings that you are doing the right thing. In this case, only God knew. I was getting tired of trying to figure it out.

Encountering Loss

Just then, we began to hear the toilet bubbling. My wife and I looked at each other. With my eyes, I reassured her that we were too blessed to be stressed. Nevertheless, it didn't stop me from looking out the window. I saw the wind swirling, but it wasn't acute at this point.

As the calls kept coming in, all I could do was *not* falter. The people on the phone were going through something dreadful. Apparently, the eye of the storm (which forms two eye walls and is the area with the most powerful elements, including the strongest winds and the heaviest rains) was heading for or had already made landfall in Biloxi.

Although I tried not to think about the church building itself, it did cross my mind to wonder how she was going to stand up during this hellacious storm. I had a sharp anxiety attack when I began to wonder if I would ever see certain people again. There was no way I could afford to think about *that* one for too long.

Before long, the wind began to gust. Out in my den, I could hear the insulation ripping apart. I ran to the den, only to see the wind opening up the ceiling as though it was prying open a stubborn can. I took a deep breath to reassure my wife that this was just a material possession. Then, we could hear the porch getting beat-up as the wind started to howl. In two to three minutes, the wind had come back to viciously smacking at the house like a girl in a wild fight, with hands flailing away like a propeller blade. Tension filled my face and the tears welled up behind my eyes. I felt my neck muscles tightening. I shook my head, determined to fight off any negativity. Sensing my wife next to me and feeling her pain, I tried to keep myself cool.

Around noon — the power went out. We didn't panic; although, we were silent on the issue. We viewed it as a *comfortable* catastrophe in light of what other folks were going through in Biloxi. However, when the water started coming in, we had no choice but to reach higher ground. With my wife by my side, I knew that we would have to be there for each other like never before — come Hell or high water.

> **In my den, I could hear the insulation ripping apart. I ran to the den only to see the wind opening up the ceiling as though it was prying open a stubborn can.**

Some people were now in the rafters while battling still rising waters. Since Katrina had brought the ocean waters onto land, she brought with her sea creatures and the like. Some particularly feared cottonmouth snakes and the fire ants that they were beginning to see in those attics. I said prayers of protection for all of them. I knew it was getting difficult for the people to stay positive, but it was a matter of survival at this point. To my dismay, no sooner than I would get off the phone, I could hear pieces of our house being ripped off. I remained composed, but this thing was starting to sprout mold in my soul. This not-knowing-the-outcome feeling was starting to vex my spirit.

He wasn't surprised with what I was going through, and I encouraged myself by knowing that God's Presence is with us all the time; I had to keep telling myself that even though my emotions said something else, such as, *Where are You?*

As if they were playing tag, positive and negative thoughts kept exchanging places. I seemed to have the external issues

PRIVATE PAIN

under control by putting on a brave face, but I knew the internal problems would be far more difficult to handle, especially when by 6:00 P.M., my yard was blanketed with shingles and the water was rising in my backyard to about 4-ft. deep. Yet some were literally up to their necks in it back in Biloxi. It made no sense grieving for myself, when obviously others had it far worse.

As we made ourselves content to camp out in the hot, wet, and dark house, with only flashlights and candles for light, we knew that if worse came to worse, we had enough food and water to last several days. If the water rose any higher, then it would have to be the same route as others — to the attic and then to the roof. Of course, that wouldn't happen, since my house was not situated in a flood-prone area.

The kids used to have a statement called "Recognize — you better recognize" to try to make you understand where they were coming from. They wanted you to get a picture of what they were saying, so that, along with them, you could be on the same wavelength. Realizing that there was a lot at stake, and knowing that it was not easy, I began to "recognize" that I am an imperfect man holding the key to Heaven — 'Faith'.

In fact, there was no other way to deal with the situation, other than to accept it for what was — Chaos.

More people were desperate and were hanging on for their dear lives. Some were hanging in trees, some were nestled in the corner of attics, and some were floating on top of freezers while dealing with water moccasins and anything else that Katrina drug in from the Gulf. Some managed to make it out of collapsing structures and make their way onto the rooftops of floating houses. Upon hearing these stories in real-time, it's hard to shut off your heart valve, because you know the body count is increasing as you speak to them.

Dr. DeBruce Nelson

Watching our situation at home go from bad to worse, I had to lock my rage in a cage. The same way you have to do when you hear that other countries, supposedly not as rich as ours, have some form of universal health care. The dissonance between what was happening in Alabama and what was happening in Biloxi was too much for me to rationalize. I simply prayed for The Lord to be a guide and shield on *this* battlefield.

> So when one of the saints told me they were stuck in a tree infested with fire ants, I took a gulp and shook my head.

As for *battlefields*, the people back in Biloxi were struggling for life and limb. It seems as though Katrina had kicked up the entrenched fire-ant population. These longstanding nuisances have no natural predators. So when one of the saints told me they were stuck in a tree infested with fire ants, I took a gulp and shook my head. These fire ants were biting them all over. And to add insult to injury, there were people, knowingly petrified by snakes, who were forced to deal with water moccasins staring them in the face. On top of that, some people were battling water as waves persisted in smashing them in the face. Just imagine someone continuously throwing water in your face. Not only would you be mad that they wouldn't stop, but you'd be upset at their utter cruelty to your person.

In the dark irony, some people were forced to fight off rats clinging to them because they were scared of Katrina, not knowing that the human had one up on them; they were scared of rats. One person was hanging onto a light pole, another hanging in a tree overlooking the church's kitchen, wondering when he was going to eat again or if he would be alive to ever eat again.

The next story shook me more than words can say. It shook me similar to seeing people on a National News Show catch on fire due to using their cellphones while pumping gas; I made a mental note to never do that. Whether it was television hype or not, it was enough to make me think twice, and ultimately review the things I do. Having said that, one of the saints I was talking to was hanging up in a tree. He saw a man dipping under the waves and resurfacing again, so he calmly said to me, "Hold on, Pastor, 'cause I gotta go save this drowning man. Pray for me." The next thing I heard was the phone hitting the water.

That was an eye opener, similar to when you realize that people are going broke to look and feel good in tennis shoes. It gives you perspective. Still, even with that, I couldn't share with my wife the gravity of the situation, so I had to be very careful about how I reacted to what the people were saying. I wanted to be there for them and for my own family at the same time.

By 8:00 P.M., I could tell the storm was growing tired of her fury, because the wind gusts were coming less frequently. Right then and there, it popped into my mind to call my brother to see if he would mind going to Biloxi once the water receded. There was no way I could tell my wife what I was considering. When I looked at her, she wasn't the worse for wear, but I could tell she wasn't exactly at peace. I could tell she wanted to burst, but she was staying strong. I guess, sometimes we think it's our God-given right to complain about what we are going through, but in catastrophic situations like this, sometimes you realize that complaining is more of a stress reliever than it is a healer, similar to how people think that *obtaining* things is equal to *achieving* things. With this, I began to see Katrina as a wicked schoolmistress teaching us things that perhaps we'd taken for granted.

Sometime during the 8:00 o'clock hour, while talking, my phone cut off for good. I wasn't going to start slitting my wrists, but it was definitely salt in my wounds. I was mad at myself for feeling that; I felt dead wrong. It was as though I was showing my

Dr. DeBruce Nelson

doubt or even shaking my fist at God. I felt as though my lack of faith was blatant disrespect to God for not having unshakeable faith. To ease this feeling, I began to pray intensely that God would keep the people safe from harm and disaster. I figured that if I couldn't connect with the people physically, I could at least intercede for them spiritually. There was really no alternative; the plug on the drain had been lifted.

By this time, I felt I was afraid and okay at the same time, but whether it was in my imagination or in physical reality, I couldn't tell you. But it was a dubious feeling — however it went.

I began to ease my way outside to survey the mess, determined not to let negative stress show. However, taking in the gravity of your loss at a time like this is very unique to each person. Whatever the case, it will either hit your mind first or your heart first. When it hits your mind first, you have to be prepared for the long haul. You shake your head and reluctantly accept it. However, when it hits your heart you almost buckle, as tears, pain, and anguish wash over you.

Needless to say, my wife wasn't happy with my decision to go to Biloxi with my brother at around 11:00 p.m., but upon her understanding, she reluctantly agreed. So, my brother and I hopped into my truck and headed west on Interstate 10. The damage was increasing as we made our way. As you can imagine, the driving conditions were extremely bad, as debris was everywhere. We were forced to zigzag in two feet of water between trees and downed power lines. How much is too much? Is the price to be able to live in this Gulf Coast Paradise playground of Gulfport, Biloxi, and Mobile too high when considering this damage? The closer I got to my areas of major concern, the darker my thoughts grew. At this point, you want to try to stay positive, but your raging mind won't let you. As you can imagine, a way to keep the fear and uncertainty at bay is to be thankful for what you

PRIVATE PAIN

have. I say this, because in an uncertain situation like Katrina, you can run, but you can't hide from the destruction. It scars the area so that you cannot forget it. It looked as if a war had taken place and the area had been bombed.

We were able to drive within one thousand feet of the Lighthouse Church before we had to get out of the pickup because there were houses in the road. I took a couple of steps; my rage took a couple extra. Wading through water, I began to understand that our seven years of hard work to whip this building into tip-top shape had disappeared in the minute the water had come in and decided it wanted to stay for a while. Sensing the devastation, despite trying to set my mind straight, I stood there, numb, telling myself that this was all a bad dream, even if the reality was undeniable.

The tears wanted badly to flow, but although my eyes watered, I could not grant them leave. Although she was still back at our house, I could see Janet's face in front of me. Those soft brown eyes, that tender face.

The closer we got, the worse the devastation appeared. Half of the homes were gone. Half of the trees were horizontal. There were no road signs or traffic lights. We passed several houses that appeared whole from a distance, however, as we drew alongside, we could see that the ground floors contained no glass, no doors, and no possessions. Homes were gutted out, leaving behind just concrete slabs. The roads were covered in lumber, shingles, furniture, clothes, and a little bit of everything else. Cars and trucks were in piles like toys tossed in a box. It was clear that streets and homes were flooded as far as six miles inland.

When we came back the next morning, with my wife, we saw busy National Guardsmen and Red Cross Disaster Relief workers rescuing people and getting people out of stranded areas. Seeing them, we knew we needed to be careful.

Dr. DeBruce Nelson

I wasn't sure that my wife was hearing me, so I turned around. In shock, she was busy looking over the devastation, seeing how many memories were drowned in the water. I'm sure that, like me, her mind was all over the place. I saw her eyes brimming with tears, and then a wide one rolled down her cheek.

I felt overwhelmed. Seeing my wife in pain made praise very difficult. All the gold in the world is not worth seeing her in that state. Knowing her need for security and to see this mess, makes that heathen rage want to come out. Like people running away from raging bulls, thoughts just go all over the place. I wondered how well the church had held up. I wondered if such and such's house was okay. Who had died? How had they died? Will I have a church? Is there a church? The images of all the people I had spoken to on the phone kept coming back like a repeating commercial. I could see people hollering in attics, others hanging in trees, and many people essentially caught up in life and death situations.

> **Sensing the devastation, despite trying to set my mind straight, I stood there numb telling myself that this was all a bad dream, even if, the reality was undeniable.**

It was more akin to a bomb having been dropped, as opposed to the rising waters of New Orleans that had created a different sort of problem.

My heart filled with sadness for old East Biloxi, because, to me, she is Biloxi. She is the oldest neighborhood in the city and represents what we are, a close-knit community of large extended families and individuals. People have lived here for generations. And although it's a poor community, Blacks, Whites, and in-betweens come together to make up its population.

PRIVATE PAIN

Many families have lived here for generations, and a sense of community is apparent on the street because we all know each other. The thoughts of the pain of what the saints may be feeling ran through me. Some of these people were a major part of me. Some of them were so familiar that we could finish each other's sentences. We knew each other more than just by name.

As an individual, as well as a member of a team, I see myself as being thoughtful and community minded. Right then and there, it occurred to me that if the renaissance does occur, it could be a much needed springboard to a more balanced life for some folks around here.

Seeing all of this, as much as you want to know, the truth is, you don't really want to know. It was clear that my life had changed and that I was going to never be the same. Before you dismiss that as an overstatement, imagine this: You come home from work today, and not only is your house totally destroyed, but your whole *neighborhood* is totally destroyed.

Knowing that, we decided to visit God's House first and foremost. Driving down Division Street, one could tell that Katrina smacked here real hard, too. Despite the fact that we were a mile from the waterfront and in an official "No Flood Zone", Katrina was too hardheaded to care about our designer labels or our man-made distinctions. However, before we got there, I had to give God praise because I could see that the Lighthouse was still standing.

We got out of the car and immediately noticed that the entire town smelled of decomposing garbage. We covered our mouths, because the foul stench pervaded the air to the point of burning your throat. Then you ask yourself, *Is this what human decay smells like?*

The cracked streets were full of debris and still contained filthy water. No doubt, this place was a public health nightmare. Going in, the water had practically receded, but you could see a watermark where it had flooded 13 feet up to the second floor.

Seeing the devastation, I knew it was outside the realm of understanding. Thinking back on 9/11, it was clear to me, as I remembered then, that the first few days of any disaster response is characterized by absolute chaos. Then, the Holy Spirit reminded me that God made this world out of chaos. Empowered by that reminder, we went to visit some of the saints who had been trapped in attics. Upon reaching them, many were shaking in fear. I kept repeating, "It's gonna be alright."

After getting these saints to the makeshift shelters set up by the Red Cross, we made our way back. On the way back, God would perform a miracle for us. It occurred while we were driving on a straight stretch — and the road gave way. We went airborne, and if we had landed on anything else other than on the other side of the broken stretch of road, only God knows what would've happened. As it was, we somehow stayed airborne long enough to land on the other side, just like "General Lee", the car in *The Dukes of Hazard*.

Chapter Two
COPING WITH TRAGEDY

"The worst thing about grief is the length of time during which the experience lasts. For the first weeks one is in a state of shock. But the agony lasts long after the state of shock comes to an end. After a year, or about two, the agony gives way to a dull ache, a sort of void. During the night in one's dreams, and in the morning when one wakes, one is vaguely aware that something is wrong and, when waking is complete, one knows exactly what it is." — Lord Halisham of St. Marylebone, A Sparrow's Flight.

Dr. Nathan Kollar, Professor of Religious Studies at St. John Fisher College, offered these words on suffering: "Like a tree struck by lightning—splintered, shaken, denuded—our world is broken by suffering, and we will never be the same again."

No doubt, most people have found the devastation of Hurricane Katrina to be unbelievably horrible. It has caused many to be fearful, tearful, and sorrowful. These emotions are intensified by the feelings of helplessness which accompany the shock from the impact of this horrific natural disaster and the many man-made incidents which have occurred in its aftermath. It is normal to have difficulty managing your feelings after major tragedies because everyone experiences stress differently.

A natural disaster, such as a hurricane, not only leaves a trail of property destruction in its wake, but, many times, it leaves thousands of its victims with a destroyed sense of balance. Victims may need to devote time to restoring their own sanity. It is very important to be extra patient and to accept that physical and emotional healing is a process. In a crisis situation, it is essential to have a supportive network with family, friends, and neighbors.

According to the National Mental Health Association, in coping with stress caused by a disaster, one needs to open up. By talking with others about the event, you can relieve stress and realize that others share your experiences and feelings. Secondly, there is a need to spend time with friends and family members. They can help you through this tough time. If you have children, encourage them to share their feelings and concerns with you. Also, it helps a great deal to take one thing at a time. Getting things back to normal can seem impossible; however, when one breaks the job into double tasks, completing each task will give you a sense of accomplishment and make things seem less overwhelming.

Seven Years of Toiling, Over Within Twelve Hours

What would you do if a hurricane came and took away everything you had? And you had no food, no water, no clothes, only your life. I say that because it was clear that Katrina was a flat-out leveler. And, ironically enough, just as the reality hit me that Katrina came in waves, it was beginning to dawn on me that the recovery, too, was going to have to come in waves.

Tuesday, August 30, 2005 was the second day of hurricane Katrina. Be that as it may, I hadn't slept in 24 hours, and I saw no sleep in sight. With that in mind, there was no sense in getting a shovel to dig my own grave. At this point, it was all about putting in work. Convinced of that, I spent most of my time clearing debris from the House of God and wondering where stuff was. As I was picking up the pieces, I realized that there were so many Old Time Proverbs amongst this mess. Out of the many, the one I will reveal was Psalm 23.

PRIVATE PAIN

The fact that all in my household were alive and accounted for was a blessing. And considering the near devastation of everything I witnessed in Biloxi on the previous night, we had better count our blessings, as far as the damage went. To some degree, I was glad that we were able to minimize the damage by grabbing things and moving them upstairs. Even though, some of the stuff that we placed around in the building on the tops of tables and such were ruined.

As it went, we were still without power, and the telecommunications were null and void.

We were without landlines and cellphones. But it didn't matter, because it was all about taking one step at a time. During this painstaking time, I would look at Janet and her head was hung low. She wasn't crying, but her "I can't believe this" headshakes were full of dry tears. Knowing that this was a time of mercy and healing, I prayed silently for God to show us that He was still in control. Then I said, "Baby, I know this is overwhelming. I know you're tired and burdened right now, but we've got to give this bill to Him. We have to keep the faith, no matter what."

Going from room to room, there were times when we both stopped for a moment, stunned in disbelief that the place where we worshipped was reduced to this moldy mess.

My wife nodded as though she understood, but I could tell that a large part of her was gone. I took a step toward her, cocking my head to the side to gauge if she was okay. Even if she said nothing, it didn't matter to me; it was written all over her face. Looking into her tender brown face, I could tell there was an avalanche of pressure on her, ready to fall, but she surprisingly said, "He is... in control, and I know, He's gonna bring some good out of this."

I shook my head with a smile, and like the old troubadours who sang love songs to the apple of their eye, my heart sang to Janet the melody that my mouth couldn't utter. She was my helpmate, for sure. She was the one who opened my heart, allowing me to rise above my own self-interest, and allowing me to love her more than I loved cooked food. If I were a knight in the Middle Ages fighting for the love of my Janet, someone would be dead, and it wouldn't be me.

Having said that, I didn't want to dash her hopes for rebuilding by reminding her that we didn't have flood insurance. It wasn't the time and place to mention it, although I knew the issue would be hovering over us like an inky sky, ready to rain when it felt ready. Going from room to room, there were times when we both stopped for a moment, stunned in disbelief that the place where we worshipped was reduced to this moldy mess. Still, we kept on picking up the pieces. After going through the building and surveying the scene, we turned our attention to the outside. Once outside, although it was bright and sunny, the building looked like someone had thrown a grenade into it.

Here We Go Again

On my way back to Biloxi that afternoon, along with my brother, I sped through while telling myself that no matter what, I was going to be a faithful and loyal soldier in doing my duty. As I did, boy-oh-boy, you sure can see things a lot clearer in the light of day. The closer I got to Biloxi, the clearer the destruction was becoming, and the harder it hit. No doubt, to use a boxing metaphor, Katrina had decided to test our chins to see if it was easy to knock us out. In seeing this hot mess, I kept trying to compare things to Katrina.

Katrina was like Oprah Winfrey's character, Sofia, in *The Color Purple*, before she lost her steam. Sofia was clearly determined

PRIVATE PAIN

not to take a backseat to anyone, just to get along, as she was meant to rule and not take orders. Not only was she not afraid to fight against the odds, she was willing to raise hell if she had to — whatever it took to make her presence felt.

Stated simply, Katrina was a leveler, leveling low-rise buildings and leaving many with only the foundation.

She came in kicking butts and taking no names. She twisted, curled, and broke up roads like it was nothing. You'd see the rubble among fallen trees, downed power lines, and smashed cars and appliances. She smashed storefronts to rubble and swept whole neighborhoods from one side to the other. She also threw some of them into the Gulf. She even used the Gulf against some of them, as she took the barges that the casinos were built upon and slammed them into the coast.

Places like the Tivoli Hotel had torn-away barges slammed repeatedly against it, knocking out part of the first four floors.

Dr. DeBruce Nelson

The telltale signs of the true destruction came when seeing the casinos. High-rise casinos near where Interstate 10 hits the shoreline were largely intact above the second or third floor. Below that, many were see-through, as they were unable to survive relentless winds. Oddly enough, some of the most severe damage in Mississippi was inflicted upon the beachfront houses of the wealthy.

PRIVATE PAIN

Before Katrina

After Katrina

Dr. DeBruce Nelson

One thing which became steadily clear was that Biloxi was never going to be the same.

Funny enough, the iconic Hard Rock Café sign continued to strum as Katrina hit her, even though the building behind it was smashed. Just knowing that so many infrastructures which had survived Hurricane Camille couldn't stand up to Katrina got me to wondering.

Apparently, unlike big bad Camille who had come with much higher winds that shattered windows with the snap of a finger, Katrina brought with her wind-driven, pounding waves on top of her storm surge. In Biloxi, she combined with Back Bay to batter us. It was as if after gathering everyone together, she positioned herself between two columns, and in all her strength she pushed until the arena fell.

In an attempt to compare Katrina to Camille, when Camille hit, she was beady-eyed and creating a 25-foot storm surge that stretched from the center outward for 120 miles. However, Katrina was wide-eyed, creating a 28-foot storm surge that stretched out over 300 miles. Katrina, the new standard for destruction, has forever changed the boundaries for how hurricanes will be measured. She set the trend that the rest will follow. I think that was her intent.

Characteristic	Camille	Katrina
Category at landfall	5	4-5
Winds at landfall	190 mph	140 mph
Pressure at landfall	26.84 inches	27.11 inches
Diameter of eye at landfall	10 miles	32 miles
Storm Surge	25 feet	20-30 feet

PRIVATE PAIN

No disrespect to anyone in New Orleans or Louisiana for their portion of Hurricane Katrina, however, Biloxi and Gulfport got hit too. I don't blame anyone for not knowing where we are. Some in Mississippi consider us part of Louisiana anyway.

Nonetheless, New Orleans, because it is below sea level and was mainly damaged by the flooding after the levees collapsed, was only brushed by the western side of the storm. However, Katrina's strongest winds hit the Mississippi Coast. Biloxi and Gulfport got the worse of it, because we were in that eastern side of Katrina, the most feared part of the storm.

By all accounts, the area of our church, poverty-stricken East Biloxi, was hit hardest by Katrina's 30-foot storm surge coupled with 140-mph winds.

Sadly, when it hits you that you are driving through a trash dump that isn't *gonna* clear up no time soon, it's like seeing an avalanche coming down on you, and you throw your balled fist at it while saying, "Go on and kill me; I can't take no more anyway."

Out of that pensive mood, you think about the times you've been to the landfill or a junkyard. Unless you work there, you go in there and just get what you want. You are not trying to stay in that mess and filth. And even when you see the workers at work there, you wonder how much they are getting paid to put up with that mess. Sensing and thinking this, fear immediately tried to put a chokehold on me, but I shook it off with, *If God is by my side, what can be against me?*

Depleted Community

The thing about Biloxi is that it is 70 miles northeast of New Orleans, 70 miles southwest of Mobile, and 150 miles west of Jacksonville, Florida. It is a 300-year-old fishing town-turned-casino magnet where gaming revenues had accounted for more than a third of its annual budget. In East Biloxi, before Katrina, many were wrestling with issues of crime, drug activity, low incomes, lack of employment opportunities, affordable housing, and a struggling local economy.

Back in East Biloxi, seeing the cars on top of houses and both of them in the middle of the street, it hit me that this was by far the greatest devastation I'd ever seen — no doubt! It look like a scene from *Night of The Living Dead*, because people were walking around in the streets like zombies, obviously homeless, because they had nowhere to go, nothing to eat, nothing to drink, and from what I saw, no one to help them. I'm sure the Red Cross was around somewhere, no doubt overtaxed, but I didn't see them around at that time.

Instead, I saw whole families walking around dazed and confused. Some had a bag or two over their shoulder, and some were carrying around a family heirloom or two. I had never seen so much blank confusion in human eyes except on television. It was as though these families had survived the worst natural disaster in history, but now they wondered how they were going to survive after the storm. And with their lives being totally upended, I could tell that this situation was going to become more than dire.

The jaw-dropping images that were being burned into my memory as I walked around were, where there were once houses, now there was only debris and the scattered belongings of residents. I saw some people sifting through piles of clothes and lifetime possessions amongst the rubble. Seeing this, I searched for some way to truly convey what happened here. I'm sure I'm not doing justice to it even now.

Nevertheless, looking at so many homes having been obliterated, it dawned on me that human beings are partly creatures of habit and conformity. Like Janet and I, people love their little homes, and they get used to them. After all, so many people leave their houses in a complete mess, that to the outsider the place needs to be cleaned up thoroughly, but to that person, they plumb get use to it — probably *too* used to it. Some go as far as to say, *"At least I know where everything is; I got a system. It ain't bothering nobody but you; it's my mess."* Whether you agree or disagree with this type of thinking, it just didn't matter in this case, because these people had no homes to get used to anymore.

As I stood reflecting on what remained, it was clear that there was no turning back the clock. If that were possible, I would've kept it there. After all, the people here were so familiar with each other that they could finish each other's sentences.

As I stood there, my gag reflex was on overdrive because of the foul stench which pervaded the air. It smelled like one of those stink bombs that people used to let off in school. I really needed a gas mask, because the smell was burning my eyes and making me constantly clear my throat.

What perplexed me the most was that this wasn't the best neighborhood in the world, but how could they ever recover from this? Just thinking about it, I kept massaging my eyeballs, trying to keep the tears in their place. If I ruled the world, I would assure these people that anything that could be replaced, would be. Since I couldn't give that, I encouraged them to simply keep the faith.

Walking amongst the people, searching their Black, White, and yellow anxious, shell-shocked, and dragged-in-from-the-mud faces, I could tell that they were angry, frustrated, blinking rapidly, and trying to shield their eyes from the bright sun. I'm sure that the high heat and humidity was filling their cup to their brim, and by doing that, it was adding to the fight against frustrations. Their weather-beaten fight was more than visible, as quite a few had untreated cuts and bruises. Not meaning to make light of their pain, but many were equally shouting at the Devil and fussing at God. Amidst the chaos and growing tension, I had to pick my spots carefully about telling them to look to God despite the mess they saw.

By in large, though, many were cussing and fussing about being left in this squalor while being residents of the richest country in the world. I hate when people say this type of stuff, because it just goes to show that it takes tragedies like this to show that we ain't ever been equal in this country.

Of course, the most disquieting aspect of seeing this desperation for me lay in knowing that I still had to pay the piper, because in the back of my mind, I still had the haunting images from the previous night in my head. Then, I was in a quest to find out who had survived and who hadn't. It was indeed a state of emergency, and I had been forewarned that the end would not be pretty. At this, I began to inquire about certain people. I found that some people had sought refuge at Biloxi High School, which was used as a last-resort shelter.

When some of them saw me, they gave me one of the returning-from-war-type of hugs. They were filled with longing and thankfulness. I felt the joy and pain in their soul-relieving laughs.

"I'm glad to see you, too," I kept telling people.

When I came across two sisters, they looked pain stricken. Looking at the grief in their eyes, as they just shook their heads, the blank stare was as though they were looking past me into the scene that was causing so much distress. They told me of their brother losing his wife.

Right there I gave thanks to God, because against this backdrop, it was harder to imagine any greater loss, knowing how much I loved my wife. I promised that I would help them.

The only other death which had occurred was that of the young man in the wheelchair. Apparently, he had strapped himself into his wheelchair. The authorities found him dead, still strapped into the wheelchair. Upon hearing this news, I wiped the sweat off of my forehead, wondering how many more had to suffer and die. I didn't want to know the answer.

As I continued to survey the aftermath, I wished I could have been an instant repairer of the situation. Deep inside, I thought of a way to end the misery, before I dismissed it as foolish. Seeing the lack of pastors on the scene, it crossed my mind as to how many had cut and run, and when or if they were coming back. Regardless, I could tell that many late-night contemplations were being phased into this recovery game. Especially considering the stark reality that the vast majority of these people didn't have the right insurance; after all, property insurance generally doesn't cover losses from floods, meaning that many would be without resources to replace what had been lost. Though the Federal Government provides insurance for flood losses, many, and in particular the poorer residents, do not have this coverage. Like us in Alabama, many in Mississippi did not have insurance to cover flood damage.

On top of the chaos, it was clear that there were other issues which were bound to creep up, considering the environmental health conditions such as human waste, toxins, and hygiene. The place was literally a cesspool, making a second disaster possible, mainly, the long-term health of people who have been dehydrated, starved, deprived of medication, and marooned in these filthy, filthy conditions.

The whole scene was piercing through my soul, as I kept taking deep breaths while trying to stave off that same feeling of hopelessness which I saw in so many other faces. It seemed to me that since we had survived this unprecedented natural disaster, we were going to have an unprecedented response. The reality reflected in this degradation was the knowledge that behind this devastation lay an opportunity to serve God in a way which the situation called for. Thinking about that, I said to myself, I'll be living proof that God is a redeemer and a deliverer. I stayed to help and witness to as many people as I could.

A Chance To Make A Difference

Every individual will experience crises. In fact, crisis situations often reveal one's ability to succeed — and to survive. Some people are better than others at coping with crisis situations. Those people who cope well with crises are the ones who don't wait for the crisis to strike before they can prepare themselves. Several years ago, a young girl, Ann Kiemel, wrote a book entitled, *I'm Out to Change My World*, and in this book she said, "I'm just an ordinary woman, an ordinary girl from an ordinary background, but I'm out to change my world." And then she did, through her life, her books, her speaking, and by beginning an organization to help hundreds of needy, neglected children.

The reason why God created us and placed us here in the world is because He wants us to make an impact for Him in our homes, our neighborhoods, and in our churches. By the Grace of God and the Power of God in my life, I crave to make an impact in my surroundings. Titus 2:14 says, *"Christ died for the purpose of making us his very own, different kind of people, ambitious to do worthwhile things."* I'm ambitious to please God. I want to be God's 'agent of change' in a sick, sad, and dying world. I want to make an impact for God!

A story is told of a family in Knoxville, Tennessee, who saw their beautiful home utterly destroyed by fire. A neighbor came over to console them and said, "Oh, this is terrible. You've lost everything." And the man smiled and said, "No, we still have the important things." As he put his arm around his wife, he said, "We still have each other; we have our precious children, and we have our faith in God." That's a different value, isn't it?

Probably you may ask, "What can one person do? The problems of society are so vast!" The answer is that one person can do a lot. Every great movement started with one person and moved forward because of individuals. A great many people are doing something to help the homeless, in churches and in volunteer programs all across the world.

There are numerous examples in history where a single person of courage changed the course of events. Be it Nelson Mandela, Mahatma Gandhi, Martin Luther King Jr., or Mother Teresa, they all used their patience, perseverance, compassion, and self-confidence to stay put on the path they had chosen.

Thinking about my next move got me into thinking about the character of the great ordinary leaders who rose from the average to make a difference in their surroundings. I wanted to be part of the solution and not part of the problem. I realized that the pressure to meet expectations can seemingly beat you down. It makes you question one of the most used but seldom understood terms: character, a common thread in all heroes. What do you do when no one is looking? What do you do when there is nothing to gain? Despite living in a culture which seems vain, internal qualities have to be just as important as obvious ones. Nevertheless, we tend to judge each other on the basis of what we perceive the other does. We never seem to dig deep enough. To me, I agree somewhat with the statement, "Character is born more than it is worn." But more than that, I believe that with God, all things are possible.

Thinking about *character* got me to thinking about my school days. Too often, you never really knew the teacher by gauging them in the classroom. You tended to get a fuller picture of them outside of the classroom setting. It happened during passing periods, athletic events, and trips to the grocery store. Students evaluated the way teachers interacted with other teachers, with people in the community, and with their families. Therefore, for a student to truly trust and respect teachers, they had to believe that the teachers were sincere — in word *and* deed. The teacher wasn't telling you to do something because they themselves had violated the law. Students had to believe that the teachers were modeling the same behavior in their professional lives which reflected their personal lives. Nowadays, with all of these teachers missing the mark, it makes you wonder if they truly have *character*. But what does that *really* mean?

We all know that *character* can have positive or negative associations. For instance, when someone is called "A person of character," it usually refers to a positive quality. It means they're supposed to be ethically and morally upright and capable of being trusted. When someone is said to have *little character* or a *dark character*, these are negatives. When someone is just *a character*, it means that he or she is unique. They could be funny, silly, interesting, way out there, or just plain crazy. Whatever the case, there is something about them that makes them stand out.

Whether it's mentioning Mother Teresa, Nelson Mandela, Martin Luther King Jr., or Rosa Parks, all these names stand out in history, because each one of them made an impact in their lifetime and left legacies that prevail to this day.

These ordinary people did extraordinary things to change the world, and they show us that we all have legacies to leave. Our legacies may never be written about in an encyclopedia or documented in the news. But we have the power to make our lives not only memorable for ourselves as we live it, but also for others who look back on it.

Each one of us has the potential to do with our lives what we wish. The image, thoughts, and impacts we have left behind are an indication of how we have spent our lives. We shouldn't wait until history tells our story to make a legacy; we have the opportunity to do it now. *Character* is forged in the flames of adversity. Done right, suffering can fuel greatness.

The Drive To Overcome

Imagine the plight of a boy who had a hearing problem and so could not understand his teacher's instructions well. He was labeled a mentally weak child who had no brains for studies and was thrown out of the school! This child was none other than the great Thomas Alva Edison. Now, would you agree with the school that he was dumb? How is it possible, then, for a dumb child to patent more than 1000 inventions — more than the collective patents of all the scientists of his time? There is something to be said about an inward force which drives our lives to beat the odds and causes us to triumph in the midst of troubles.

Great players step up in the face of adversity. One of them, John Elway, a former football quarterback in the National Football League (NFL) for the Denver Broncos from 1983 through 1998 said of his greatest heroic victories, "Great quarterbacks make great plays in great games. That's what it's all about, isn't it?" Elway made that statement after the game known as "The Drive". In this game, Elway was quarterbacking the Denver Broncos against the Cleveland Browns in the AFC Championship Game. The game that decided who would go to the Super Bowl.

John Elway had a basic game plan, "We don't look at the situation. We look at what we can do about the situation."

Dr. DeBruce Nelson

In the Cleveland Browns' old, decrepit stadium, on a cold, muddy field, and with a 5-degree wind chill, Elway and crew had their backs against the wall. Trailing 20-13 with 5½ minutes left in the fourth quarter, Denver took over on their two-yard line on a 100-yard field. Doing the math, that's 98 yards away from the tying touchdown.

Elway said in interviews later on that it suddenly flashed in his mind that it was time to step up and become great. Elway, who had already proven himself as a come-from-behind quarterback, engineered the heroic comeback by keeping this game tight — making smart throws and scrambling at the right time. Eventually, he wielded his time deep down into his opponent's territory to the Browns' 14-yard line.

Not seeing an open man, Elway ran for 9 yards to create a third and 1 at Cleveland's 5-yard line. After hiking the ball, Elway looked to throw it to running back Gerald Willhite who was moving wide in the flats, but he was covered, so Elway fired a dart to Mark Jackson in the middle of the end zone with 37 seconds left. After the kicker made the extra point, the game was tied.

Now, in *sudden death overtime* — the phase of the game where the winner must be decided, the first team that scores win. Denver received the ball first and began marching down the field, determined not to give Cleveland a shot at taking them out. The key play during overtime also occurred with their backs against the wall. It happened on third-and-12, or in other words, put-up or shut-up time. Anyway, Elway made a wild scramble throw to Steve Watson to set up the game-winning field goal that won the game 23-20.

"It definitely put me on the map," Elway would later say. He also said, "Over time, you learn when the right time is and when the wrong time is, and you try to eliminate the bad plays that you do make, while trying to make the good plays."

What Elway's heroics show us on a spiritual level is that the pressure is in the comeback, and that in order to make this comeback, you have to get your mind right — you have to have it firmly made up before you move forward. In this way, the apparent dangers you see are only as bad as you make them out to be.

In the midst of my troubles, I decided to have that unshakeable faith, that despite what I felt, despite what I saw, and despite the circumstances, I was going to keep moving forward. Like Elway, I was determined to showcase my character on the field of play by using the power I had in me. By the Power of the Holy Spirit, I was determined to do heavenly work amidst hellish circumstances. I was determined to tighten up my game.

Equipped with a drive to overcome, I looked around at the sea of despair, and I saw frustration ricocheting from mind to mind and from face to face. The frustration was rising among people who now found themselves refugees in their own city. My first plan of action was to make up my mind that no matter what, I was going to do my best to keep my smile from being locked away. I wanted to be a walking, living epistle.

With a new mindset, I started my journey over the hot coals. From my understanding, during these tragic times, basic logistics can get fouled up; communications systems can get paralyzed; a thousand urgent needs must be triaged; a vast number of well-meaning but tunnel-visioned federal, state, and local agencies, plus private charitable organizations and volunteers of EMS personnel, to utility crews, doctors, nurses, rush in to provide relief, and local elected officials are forced in front of cameras to inform and reassure the affected population. Understanding the specific gaps between the governmental bureaucracies, I knew that my church and I could become gap fillers.

Knowing that one of our problems nowadays is that people don't think ahead and that they only think for the moment, I had to realize that God had the power to strengthen what remains — us, the people — not just material stuff. With that mindset, we were thankful that the white-painted brick of the Lighthouse had indeed remained standing, even if our bus had been submerged in the storm. There was no time to mope when we stepped inside and saw the instant chaos. *Jesus is the secret, the best-kept secret.* Inside, the stained walls marked where the storm surge had peaked two feet from the ceiling. The floors and furniture were covered with mud and sludge with the pews perched on top of each other.

> **I looked around at the sea of despair and I saw frustration ricocheting from mind to mind, from face to face. The frustration was rising among people who now found themselves refugees in their own city.**

For me, I wasn't going to have a "The grass is always greener on the other side" mentality. You can't always find the cause in effect. Sometimes you have to work with what you have. Sometimes it boils down to simply "Sink or Swim". And because of that, since we were on hard-hit Division Street, it was time to turn the Lighthouse into a relief center. With that, I was ready to work with whomever. It wasn't about any one church; it was about God, and it was about doing His Word. It was up to us churches to play a major part in the rebuilding. We were determined to bring this area back to normal. We were the ones who had to come together for the sake of the people and for the Glory of God. With that, I began to get goose pimples. I had an idea. It came into my mind, something from the book of Ezra 2:68-69, *"When they arrived at the house of the LORD in Jerusalem, some of*

PRIVATE PAIN

the heads of the families gave freewill offerings toward the rebuilding of the house of God on its site. 69 According to their ability they gave to the treasury for this work..."

Right then and there, I began my street ministry, on the streets, making myself fully available to the people. I was determined to listen attentively, while hoping to redirect that negative energy which was so heavy on the scene. I started touching, listening, and hugging the people. I heard the same complaints over and over again. People began to complain that too much of the pre-storm warnings focused on New Orleans, but it was Mississippi that got hit with the bull's-eye. Hence, they were not happy that New Orleans, because of her sexiness, was stealing the post-Katrina spotlight and hogging the attention despite the people here being equally without tap water, toilets, telephones, gasoline, and other basic supplies.

> **On the streets, making myself fully available to the people, I was determined to listen attentively while hoping to redirect that negative energy which was so heavy on the scene.**

Standing near their rubble, I saw one lady shaking her head in despair and saying, "If we had known it was gonna be this bad, we would've left." Looking into the eyes of these desperate souls, I could see tiny flickers of light trying to come through the dark, raw, and uncut pain. At the same time, people were being alternately strong and then weepy. Some talked about rebuilding with an upbeat tone, while breaking down and weeping in the same sentence. All I could do was be a shoulder to lean on, cry on, and smack if needed — the last one was reserved for women and kids only.

On the streets, making myself fully available to the people, I was determined to listen attentively while hoping to redirect that negative energy which was so heavy on the scene.

People kept speculating, trying to make sense of it all. Some came to the sudden realization that they may have to leave their options open regarding leaving this place — possibly for good. All in all, people just kept shaking their heads while trying to see where God was in the midst of all this.

"This will be a blessing to the church," I kept telling people. "God has His way of bringing us back to Him."

Even as I was saying that publicly, in private, I had to remind myself that the race is not for the swift but for those who can endure… *I can't let the Devil get the best of me. Father, give me the strength to endure to the end. Father, I'm glad You are watching and guiding. You're my shelter in this time of trouble.*

In all this craziness, a middle-aged Black woman came to me asking in a mumbled, shaky, almost ghostly pitch how and where she was gonna live. The affected tone in her voice had that resigned-to-my-dying-fate feeling attached to it. It spoke on some level to her feeling of being almost invisible before all of this, and now this storm was about to make her completely invisible. I wanted to exhale loudly but was concerned that it would be bad advertisement for God. A haunting voice came into my mind, *No one wants to die poor, broke, and lonely.* Despite not knowing what to say, and actually feeling speechless, I knew what I believed, or, at least, I knew what I thought I believed, or thought I knew a little bit about it, at least. So I had to tell myself, *If you believe in God the way you say you do, now is the time to show and prove it.*

Nevertheless, I smacked my hands together, and while kindling them like two sticks, I said, "First things first. We are gonna find you a place to sleep, even if I gotta take you home with me. Go get your stuff, and come back and meet me at the church in an hour."

She shook her head like she understood, but she didn't move.

"Did you hear me?"

"Yeah, I heard you," she said, while nodding. "I heard you, good!"

I smiled, "Well, what's the problem?"

She raised a small plastic bag in front of her face, "This is all I got."

"Alright, alright, I'll tell you what," I said, pointing to my truck, "Go wait in my truck."

As I saw her walking toward my truck, I realized that either I was gonna make it, or I was gonna fall through.

Nevertheless, I was a little mad, but I wasn't about to start stomping my feet and throwing a tantrum. Instead, since I heard that they were giving away professional tents and cots, I had to do my best to secure some for my people or whoever needed them.

I heard that a supply center was being set up in the Wal-Mart parking lot, and I was determined to go there.

However, as I was walking to my truck, reality jumped out of the shadows and said, "Boo!" I was hit by a sudden shrill of terror, *These people can't sleep in this mud.*

Taking another step, reality kept coming out from the shadows. One of the clear-cut dilemmas was that of jobs. Getting in my truck, driving on autopilot, that was when my split-screen happened. True, these days were going to be long and difficult, but the best I could do was put on a brave face and go through — what else could I do? That said, I looked at this woman and realized that this wasn't about me, but that it was about her, and others just like her.

The thing is, no sooner than I had secured a tent and cots, I continued visiting the infirmed and distressed. One lady asked me if I could secure her some diabetic medicine or she was going to die. She was, in effect, asking me to go back through the maze and find this medicine. It would have been easier to ask me to pull a rabbit from a hat. Then, in the moment of her desperation, I recognized that God was just going to have to deliver — no ifs, ands, or buts about it. That said, I graced her hand and let her know that God was going to deliver her from her peril. I stepped away from her and walked with my body riddled with concern. I felt punch-drunk. However, as I started walking, from out of nowhere a team of nurses came by and asked me if I needed some assistance.

"Y'all got some diabetic medicine?"

"I believe so," a lady replied with a smile. "Do you need some?"

I pointed in the direction of the old mother who needed it, "A church member of mine needs some."

"Let's go!"

Call it a coincidence or a miracle. But when you weigh it on the scales of life or death, it weighs heavily in the favor of being a lifesaver. Give me *that* over theology, over definition, over semantics, over religion, over piety, and over self-righteousness any day. I give it up to God.

Chapter Three
THE POWER OF PAIN

According to Harry J. Gould, III, MD, PhD, a Director of the Pain Mastery Center of the Department of Neurology at Louisiana State University, an estimated 50 million Americans suffer from chronic pain, and an additional 25 million experience acute pain as a result of surgery or injury. Many people assume they must live with pain, but this is simply not true. Most pain can be managed or greatly eased with proper pain management; however, the reality is that most pain goes untreated, under-treated, or improperly treated. With proper management, the overall health, well-being, and quality of life for millions of Americans can be improved. Pain is a message sent along the nerves to tell the brain that something is damaging the body. The brain then sends a message to the muscles or organs to take action — for example, it tells the hand to get away from what's burning it.

Everyone hurts physically. We psychologically respond to the pain by thinking, feeling, and acting. When you think about the pain and try to figure out what is causing it and why you are hurting, you experience emotional reactions to the pain. You may get angry, frightened, or frustrated by the pain. You then talk about the pain with family, friends, and co-workers who help to develop a social and cultural context for assigning meaning to your personal pain and help you take appropriate action.

Dr. Stephen F. Grinstead, an author and nationally recognized expert in preventing relapse related to chronic pain disorders and the developer of the Addiction-Free Pain Management System, states:

Biological pain is a signal that something is going wrong with the body. *Psychological Pain* results from the meaning that an individual assigns to the pain signal. *Social* and *Cultural Pain*, also known as suffering, results from the social and cultural meaning assigned by other people to the pain that is being experienced, and whether or not the pain is recognized as being severe enough to warrant a socially approved sick role. These three components determine whether the signal from the body to the brain is interpreted as pain or suffering. The psychological meaning applied by the mind to the physical pain signal will determine whether we simply feel pain (Ouch, this hurts!) or experience suffering (Because I hurt, something awful or terrible is happening!). Although pain and suffering are often used interchangeably, there is an important distinction that needs to be made. Pain is an unpleasant signal telling us that something is wrong with our body. Suffering results from the meaning or interpretation we assign to the pain. (*Understanding Pain* by Dr. Stephen F. Grinstead, LMFT, ACRPS, CADC-II, www.addiction-free.com)

The Purpose of Pain

One person recently made the comment that when he looked at the lives of all his friends, it seemed as if every person, now or in the recent past, was dealing with some big problem or difficult issue in his or her life. The problem could be disease, a death in the family, marital difficulties, or emotional distress, but it seemed to him as if everyone had some big issue to deal with.

Another person made a rather cynical comment. That person worried, not about the people who had big problems in their lives, but about those who hadn't yet faced a major crisis. The concern was that those who still believed that life was peaceful and free of problems would soon have that innocence taken away. Not all of

PRIVATE PAIN

us face a crisis. And for some of us, the issues which we deal with in life are open and public; for others, the issues they deal with are more private and personal.

One person said, over the tragic death of a loved one, "If there is some lesson that I am supposed to learn by something as tragic as this, I'd rather not learn it." There are events of true tragic proportion: the untimely death of a loved one, terrible and painful disease, emotional disturbance and depression, the dissolving of a marriage, abuse, hunger, and famine. If we come to believe that somehow The Lord allows or even causes these to happen so that we can learn some important lesson about life, we end up with a pretty terrible idea about God. One person made the comment about such an idea, "God is a bad teacher if He uses tragedy as His lesson plan."

Probably you ask, "Why can't our life be free from pain, suffering, and the anguish of temptation? Why can't life just be easy and enjoyable?"

It is interesting to ask these questions about The Lord's life. Why couldn't even The Lord's life, when He was on the Earth, just have been peaceful? Why did He have to suffer continual temptations, as the Writings say, temptations from the beginning of His life to the very end? Why did He have to begin His ministry by being tempted by the Devil for forty days in the wilderness? Why did He have to suffer the awful pain and anguish of the passion on the cross? Why couldn't His life have been one of simple peace and joy?

When we ask these questions about The Lord's life, the answer is obvious; He didn't come here to have a life of peace and joy. He came here with a mission to be accomplished. He came here to fight against the hells. He came here to fight for generations of men, women, and children, and for generations yet unborn. He came to fight for all of us. There was a purpose to His life, a purpose greater than Himself. And the same is true for us. We are here for our own regeneration, and we are here for a cause which is greater than ourselves. And sometimes this cause will involve pain, hardship, and temptation. God is loving and merciful, even when "for the present" He allows trials and sufferings to come into our lives. *"For we know that all things work together for good to them that love God, to them who are called according to His purpose."* (Romans 8:28)

A story is told of a man who went to a barbershop to have his hair cut and his beard trimmed. As the barber began to work, they began to have a good conversation. They talked about so many things and various subjects.

When they eventually touched upon the subject of God, the barber said, "I don't believe that God exists."

"Why do you say that?" asked the customer. "Well, you just have to go out in the street to realize that God doesn't exist. Tell me, if God exists, would there be so many sick people? Would there be abandoned children? If God exists, there would be neither suffering nor pain. I can't imagine a loving God who would allow all of these things."

The customer thought for a moment, but he didn't respond because he didn't want to start an argument. The barber finished his job and the customer left the shop. Just after he left the barbershop, he saw a man in the street with long, stringy, dirty hair and an untrimmed beard. He looked dirty and unkempt.

The customer turned back and entered the barber shop again, and he said to the barber, "You know what? Barbers do not exist!" "How can you say that?" asked the surprised barber. "I am here, and I am a barber. And I just worked on you!"

"No!" the customer exclaimed. "Barbers don't exist, because if they did, there would be no people with long, dirty hair and untrimmed beards, like that man outside."

"Ah, but barbers DO exist! What happens is that all people do not come to me."

"Exactly!" affirmed the customer. "That's the point! God, too, DOES exist! What happens is that people don't go to Him and do not look for Him. That's why there is so much pain and suffering in the world."

Deluge, Death, and Debris

Wednesday, August 31, 2005 was the third day after Hurricane Katrina had killed more than a thousand people and wrecked three large cities and dozens of smaller communities. More than half-a-million homes and businesses were destroyed, and 1.4 million people were displaced. The storm swept entire towns out to sea and let America know that despite Mardi Gras, poor people really did live in New Orleans. She broke through reinforced concrete with the power of a dozen locomotives, with the surge hitting the coast like a giant hand and scraping everything away. In effect, she created chaos.

In this chaos, you seemingly walked around with a fake smile and a fake laugh, but inside you were hurting and your energy was depleted. Have you ever felt like God has hung you out to dry — in the rain — knowing you might get moldy? Frankly I felt like Job. I felt like God had taken my life from me, as I knew it. And worse than that, it seemed as though he'd allowed Katrina to be the heavy, and had allowed her to beat up on our lives with blunt-force trauma.

Dr. DeBruce Nelson

We all know that certain songs evoke pain which is easy to hide. Watching my wife, I could tell that Katrina was one of those sad songs that just makes you cry. Her face was solemn, like one of those mean-old church ladies who hold themselves so tight because they are afraid to be loosened. I felt for her, but I also knew that it was time to be bodacious.

The hard thing for my wife was that since Katrina, my loyalties seemed divided. I could tell that she was privately pondering my absence. Under most circumstances, I would be there for her; I just saw the situation pulling me toward Biloxi. I desperately needed her to understand that this experience not only transformed the life we were living at the time, but our future as well. And there was no step-by-step manual on how to handle this type of situation. There was no way to get your game back on track other than to go out there and make it happen.

As we continued to set out straight, we knew it was mind over matter in some way, as we simply tried to salvage what we could. At the same time, we tried to pick up the pieces *mentally*. Some tough choices had to be made. We can all remember having broken something valuable, and after picking it up, you look at it to see if you can put it back together again. It goes through your mind as to whether you can make the item like new, or if you can repair it enough to make it look like it did. This is why superglue and epoxy glue are so popular when things break. But, as you know, if any of you have ever used superglue, sometimes it just doesn't do the job. And, depending on how old or precious the item, you may have to consider throwing it away or taking it to someone who can try and repair it to meet your satisfaction.

At best, since Katrina, I had spent 40% of my time at home and the rest in Biloxi. Part of the reason was that I still had haunting images from Katrina. I had been asking about certain church members and still hadn't found all who I was looking for. There were still too many unanswered questions.

The thing my wife didn't realize was that it wasn't about where you were from; it was about where you're at. And where I was — needed a lot of ministry. It was my time to get some real on-the-job experience at being a true disciple. The truth be told, when it comes to walking by faith — there is a thin line between walking it, talking it, living it, giving it, and pretending it.

Of all Jesus' parables, none has worked its way deeper into the American consciousness than the Parable of the Good Samaritan. The phrase "Good Samaritan" is used to describe any person who goes out of his way to help another. It's a theme that newspaper reporters love to feature, because it captures the readers' attention and fires the imagination.

The robbers on the Jericho Road were pretty desperate. Even if a man had little of value, they would attack him for the value of his clothing alone. But they didn't just threaten him and take his clothing. They stripped him of his clothing and then beat him, probably with wood staffs. But a Samaritan, as he traveled, came where the man was, and when he saw him, he took pity on him (Luke 10:33). *"Mercy is required of us,"* (Isaiah 58:6-7; Hosea 6:6). Jesus commands his disciples very specifically, *"Be merciful, just as your Father is merciful."* (Luke 6:36)

Love, sympathy, and mercy are motivated by needing each other, while withholding mercy is essentially an act of selfishness, or, of self-preservation.

We use statements like, "Don't talk about it; be about it," when we want to imply, "Just do it." To me, it was real out there. You could go through a month of Sundays, year after year in the course of a lifetime, and still never come close to this type of tragedy. This was so up close and personal for me that I wasn't about to throw in the towel for anybody.

Solving Problems

According to Dr. Mike Murdock of the Wisdom Center in Texas, everything in the world was created to solve a problem, "We will be remembered for one of two things, the problems we solve or the ones we create." The reason why you buy a car is to solve a transportation problem. A television solves an information problem. Every part of your body has an assignment or a problem to solve. Eyes solve the problem of seeing; ears solve the problem of hearing. Everything God created is a solution to somebody, somewhere, at sometime. Somebody once said,

> "You are a solution to somebody,
> you are a reward to someone,
> somebody needs you,
> somebody wants you,
> you are necessary to somebody, somewhere, today."

Jeremiah 1:7-8 says, *"For you shall go to all that I send you, and whatsoever I command you thou shalt speak. Be not afraid of their faces, for I am with you to deliver you, says the Lord!"*

I decided that I had to go ahead with my spirit and my gut to guide me through to help the citizens redefine their lives. That was the mindset I took back with me to Biloxi — to solve problems.

> **"We will be remembered for one of two things, the problems we solve or the ones we create."**
> **Dr. Mike Murdock**

I wanted to stand out like a varicose vein to let people know that God had soldiers on the scene. Yeah, there was the US Army and National Guard on the scene, but God had some people ready to act and show mercy on his behalf. Arriving on the scene, I was determined to make this the day to offer up my church as a relief station. I made my way over to the Wal-Mart parking lot, where I saw hundreds upon hundreds of people braving 95-degree heat to stand in line to receive Red Cross assistance for Hurricane Damage done to their homes. At the same time, Red Cross volunteers were serving an endless supply of cold juice, water, and snacks, and providing activities for the kids. They were providing medical attention to those in need and providing a listening ear to all those who wanted to tell their story.

In addition, the emergency personnel were still in full swing, as they were still venturing in, while searching, inspecting, and marking each apartment and house with their orange spray-paint lettering to serve as codes. The workers painted a large 'X' on the house front. At the top of the 'X' an official would note the day of the search (9-12). The right side would show the number of people found injured; the left contained the unit nomenclature (Miss. Guard). The bottom would indicate whether anyone died inside.

With people drowning in disappointment, they were starting to take matters into their own hands. They had made it through the storm, but it seemed as though all hell was breaking loose. With these people, no strangers to danger, there was a sense of "I don't care" in the air. People started taking baths by opening up fire hydrants. I suppose that some just wanted to wash that gook off of them.

According to British Philosopher, F. H. Bradley, "Where all is bad, it can only be good to know the worst." Well, after seeing what I began to see, this started to ring true.

To add insult to injury, there was a buzz in the air about people looting. I shook my head at this, wondering if this, again, wasn't just the media focusing on the negative. However, right before my eyes, I saw that people were starting to loot groceries from wherever they could find them in order to get something to eat. People were going around in abandoned houses looking for dry clothes. It was clear that people were still sleeping outside in the sludge.

Teamwork

It was John Wooden who said, "It is amazing what can be accomplished, when you don't care who gets the credit." Immediately, I began to see the local officials to have them assign the Lighthouse as a relief center. They set me up in conjunction with the Salvation Army who were setting up a type of one-stop shop down the street from our church on the grounds of Biloxi's Yankee Stadium. They were calling this Grand Central Station, "Compassion Central". From what they told me, they were getting set up to provide meals, food, clothes, activities for children, school tutors, house cleanup, etc. for the community members of Biloxi.

> "It is amazing what can be accomplished, when you don't care who gets the credit."
> John Wooden

Going to Compassion Central, I saw them wiring up telecommunications. They were setting up a MCI/SkyTel link. Also, they were setting up computers, two phones, and hooking their existing laptops up to the network. They were setting up RV and Salvation Army Communications trailers. Knowing that life is one big road with lots of signs, I took the camaraderie as a sign that they would assist me. That said, I signed the Lighthouse up for clean up and volunteered us to be an additional help center.

Being pumped up that this thing was coming together, I took the word to the street to let people know that we were setting up shops to provide whatever comfort we could provide. And time after time, despite the encouragement, people expressed their extreme displeasure about God letting this happen. Like the situation of the Holocaust, it was proof positive to many people that God couldn't possibly exist.

The Theology of Suffering

We don't have to be in this world long before we experience pain, failure, disappointment, frustration, or a myriad of other means of suffering which cause us to grieve. We are destined to suffer. God clearly warns us in His Written Word that we can expect trouble from the day we are born, right up to the day we die, *"Man born of woman is of few days and full of trouble."* (Job 14:1)

> *"Beloved, think it not strange concerning the fiery trial which is to try you, as though some strange thing happened unto you: But rejoice, inasmuch as ye are partakers of Christ's sufferings; that, when his glory shall be revealed, ye may be glad also with exceeding joy. If ye be reproached for the name of Christ, happy are ye; for the spirit of glory and of God resteth upon you: on their part he is evil spoken of, but on your part he is glorified. But let none of you suffer as a murderer, or as a thief, or as an evildoer, or as a busybody in other men's matters. Yet if any man suffer as a Christian, let him not be ashamed; but let him glorify God on this behalf. For the time is come that judgment must begin at the house of God: and if it first begin at us, what shall the end be of them that obey not the gospel of God? And if the righteous scarcely be saved, where shall the ungodly and the sinner appear? Wherefore let them that suffer according to the will of God commit the keeping of their souls to him in well doing, as unto a faithful Creator."* (I Peter 4:12-19)

We know that God has something planned through the suffering, but we still might wonder why He allows the suffering. No matter how great the suffering, God is always at work. The Book of I Peter tells of some principles that we can apply in our lives when trials overwhelm us. Peter was a fiery Apostle of Jesus Christ. He was given a second chance after denying Christ, and he was used mightily on the day of Pentecost to preach a message where over three thousand people were saved and baptized. After those first moments in church history, there were some tremendous times of trials and difficulties which came upon the Christians of the early church. The Roman Empire was very unfriendly to Christianity. As those early Christians began to fan out around the world, they found persecution in every city and in every situation. It is recorded in history that there were Christians burned at the stake every night in Rome. We, as Christians, go through little problems and call it suffering. In our eyes, sometimes inconveniences become our trials. Suffering, as the early Christians suffered, is a far cry from the inconveniences which we face today. When those times of trial do come our way, how can we know that God is still doing something in our lives?

Job stated in the midst of his trials, *"But he knoweth the way that I take: when he hath tried me, I shall come forth as gold," (Job 23:10.)* Suffering is common for all who live for Christ. Anyone who will truly stand up for Christ will suffer persecution. *"Yea and all that will live godly in Christ Jesus shall suffer persecution,"(2 Timothy 3:12).* If we are going to find God's Purpose during suffering, we must keep our eyes on Jesus Christ. *"But rejoice, inasmuch as ye are partakers of Christ's sufferings; that, when his glory shall be revealed, ye may be glad also with exceeding joy. If ye be reproached for the name of Christ, happy are ye; for the spirit of glory and of God resteth upon you: on their part he is evil spoken of, but on your part he is glorified," (I Peter 4:13-14).* James said, *"My brethren, count it all joy when ye fall into divers temptations," (James 1:2).*

God's purpose for suffering is further clearly explained in Romans 5:3-5,

> *". . . we rejoice in our sufferings, knowing that suffering produces endurance, and endurance produces character, and*

PRIVATE PAIN

character produces hope, and hope does not disappoint us, because God's love has been poured into our hearts through the Holy Spirit which has been given to us."

One of the first questions which comes to mind when catastrophes like Katrina happens is, "Is this the wrath of God? Is this just part of the end-times catastrophes?" God's purpose is always wrapped in His Enduring Love. At the very heart of each of God's Actions is this; whether He chooses to allow trouble to touch us or whether He chooses to withhold something we desire, His plan is to save us and give us life by helping us know and experience Him.

Now this is eternal life: that they may know you, the only true God, and Jesus Christ, whom you have sent. (John 17:3 NIV)

Nevertheless, when calamities of the nature of Katrina occur, one of the first things that you have to do is get the right concept of God. You have to understand that He is more than a frustrated daddy desperately looking for his lost kids at the mall. You must realize that although love is the highest expression of God's Goodness, it is ultimately His Power which makes him able to express that love. God is not only All-Powerful but also All-Knowing, and He understands the entire story from the end to the beginning. We don't like to hear that, because it doesn't really provide immediate comfort, unless we allow it to soak in.

> **You must realize that although love is the highest expression of God's Goodness, it is ultimately His Power that makes Him able to express that love.**

During trials, we experience the Presence of God. At these times, we humble ourselves before God and admit that we need His Presence. When adversity comes into our lives, we usually want God to do a removal job, but He desires to do an improving job. In Hebrews chapter 4, He says that He will give us grace to help in times of infirmity, *"Let us therefore come boldly unto the throne of grace that we may obtain mercy, and find grace to help in time of need."* (Hebrews 4:16)

Turning Pain into Purpose

Jennifer Hudson is a young singer who first gained notice as one of the finalists on the third season of the FOX television series *American Idol*. On April 21, 2004, Hudson became the sixth of the 12 finalists to be voted off the show, finishing the competition in seventh place. Hudson received the lowest number of votes and was voted off the *American Idol* show. She went on to star as "Effie White" in the 2006 musical film *Dreamgirls*, for which she won an Oscar, a Golden Globe, a BAFTA, and a SAG Award. Jennifer was asked how she handled the disappointment of being eliminated from *American Idol* when most people thought she should win. She admitted that it was painful and that she cried a lot, but that eventually she returned to her faith. "I chose to trust that God had a bigger plan for me than I could see at the time," she explained.

Jennifer's story is a powerful reminder of how life's disappointments may, in fact, be a preparation for something even more significant in our lives. And this belief has the best chance of coming true when you make a demonstrated commitment to learn and grow from your present day circumstances.

Everyone has a destiny. No one knows what his or her destiny is until it happens, but destiny will always be there. As you go through life, the judgment you use to make choices will leave an imprint on your fate. Marriage, Family, whatever — these are all things that will weigh heavily upon your destiny. The discoveries which you make through your own experiences and the experiences of others will help you gain perspective.

PRIVATE PAIN

With that in mind, our church became a drop-off point for food and water. Before long, we had supplies coming in from left and right. We got so many that we just stacked them up six feet high all around the outside of the building.

Every time people came by and asked if we needed some supplies or some help, I said some variation of this catchphrase, "Yes, sir/madam, I could use some help."

The only problem with all that stuff was that we had nowhere to really put it. To compound the problem, most of the people who needed it had no way to get there to get it.

Between the church, the Compassion Center, and different supply points, I just wanted to relax. Not seeing the possibility of that, I just kept going. As I did, there was one strange occurrence where I had to stop, look, and listen. It happened when I was walking down the street to the Compassion Center to get a beat on the professional tent equipment. All of a sudden, I heard some faint squeaking. I stopped and tried my best to cut out the noise of people moving to and fro. I honed in on it, and to my surprise, it was a baby bird chirping for food. Had it survived Katrina? Was it born afterward? Where was its momma?

Hearing that one wonderful bird quickened my step. After I stretched out my limps, I kept stepping with renewed purpose. I just had to get those older ladies set up in those tents. The best we could do was to secure the tents and get people some protection so that they would not be homeless. Some were already looking the worse for wear. Death was definitely on the scene like a bill collector.

If you never saw 'Death' bullying a scene, then thank God for that. I'm telling you that Death was pulling on people to come with him. Looking at some people's faces, it was clear that they were on EMPTY, and they didn't have any opportunity for refueling. They were going to ride it out until they were stopped dead. When you saw these people, all you could do was encourage them to hold on, while at the same time to pray for God to sustain them. In a way, understanding that He is the Soul Provider is probably the only comfort you can take in for solace.

Every chance I got, knowing that Death was in the atmosphere, I kept asking people to praise God with me to make sure we were holding onto our faith. Still, it seemed that many had decided that with there being nothing to stay for in Biloxi, it was time to move on. Knowing that, I stayed steadfast in proclaiming this terrible tragedy would not simply define us in a negative way. I was determined to be defined by our comeback. We had the faith to bounce back as stronger, tighter, and more caring than ever — it became our song.

The pervading question that kept going around was, "What are you going to do?" Many people simply responded, "Don't know", or — they didn't respond at all.

Have you ever been put on punishment, and while you were on it, you couldn't wait to get off it and go outside. It seemed like forever, and all you could do was focus on the negative and the fact that you were a victim.

That said, while I was working upstairs, I heard yelling and obscenities. I went to the window to see what was happening. There was an impatient man forcing his way and beginning to tear down the tent. He grabbed large can goods and threw them at the people's cars.

He started yelling, "She has enough!"

He grabbed the woman, which forced me to restrain him until the police arrived to remove him from the site. He was making racial remarks at the Asians.

"We're here to meet the needs of everyone."

Later on, I began to think about the causes of human aggression. From what I gathered from my studies, there are several main causes. The first is differences among people that they can't rise above, whether it is physiological differences or that of early childhood experiences. Secondly are sociological approaches, aggression in social factors such as family and social conflicts. Thirdly are power relations where aggression arises as a function for controlling one group by another. Fourthly are straight-up aggressions which can be a part of the genetics of human nature, but this one is arguable in that aggression is not seen in all individuals, but only in some. Aggression is multidimensional and is not due to any single event; various factors contribute to it, and various scenarios bring it to fruition.

We all hold aggressive instincts, and we all deal with them differently. Some talk their way through it. Some hold it in and allow it to build up so that it explodes when that person feels threatened or is being attacked. Others may say that aggression is a learned behavior that comes from TV, violent music, from being socialized around thuggish environments, or from watching individuals get rewarded for aggressive behavior. On one hand, any type of frustration can end up with an aggressive response. On the other hand, it can have a good side, because since it is needed to survive, some may use it to drive themselves each and everyday by using it to guide them for food, water, shelter, and mating.

That understood, like Christ on Resurrection Sunday, I was ready to be revived. I figured that even if Katrina came in and tried to rule things, God forbid that she would rule over me. So, concerned about East Biloxi and Point Cadet, which we also called "The Point", I decided to get into my truck and do a little patrolling, armed with the knowledge that hundreds of people were sleeping on the ground next to the rubble of their homes, or that they were living in tents that poked out from piles of debris.

As I drove around, more tractor trailers of food and water were pulling into the parking lots of Wal-Mart, Home Depot, and the like. Unlike our church though, these tractor-trailers were guarded by dozens of lawmen. On my way back to the church, I began to wonder exactly what a church was, *Is it a building where people worship every Sunday, or is it defined by the actions which people of faith take in their community?*

I choose the latter, but either way, I had all night to think about it. I did think on it some more as well, because how are a lot of these people ever going to rebuild their lives in Biloxi? It seemed to me that there were distinct phases to this Katrina aftermath: Rescue! Relocation! Reconstruction! The last one had me concerned, because it had displacement written all over it. The rumor going around was that in order to receive a trailer from FEMA (Federal Emergency Management Agency), one had to be at their residence. Or in this case, a slab or pile of rubble, because as you already know, the vast majority of the homes in East Biloxi, especially around The Point or Back Bay, were uninhabitable.

Chapter Four
STRUGGLING TO SURVIVE

Four days after Katrina, every turn revealed more of the same — more destruction, more debris, more dead bodies being unveiled. Do you have what it takes to overcome the vicissitudes (the peaks and valleys) of life? Especially on the downside were — the cynical stares, the daily slights, the economic setbacks, and the backbiting of mankind in order to become something more than what you currently are. In a disaster, where do your first thoughts turn to? God? A loved one? A book? The Good Book? A pick-me-up stimulant? Or do you humble yourself in the valley?

I ask that question because I kept pondering it myself. The whole Katrina ordeal had me constantly questioning purpose. I believe firmly in Divine Assignment, and I kept waiting for my new assignment. In the meantime, I was doing what I could. Still, it didn't stop me from reflecting on what was going on — didn't stop me from searching for deeper meaning. To me, this situation had to be more than just paying my dues. I began to understand the statement "Ignorance is bliss", a saying that I believe could be a human condition. The truth is that it is a lot easier to turn a blind eye to situations than to be fully informed or educated about what's really going on. Frankly, it cuts down on the stress. For that reason, probably, I admit that I was never fully educated on the fact that those things which unite us are stronger than those which divide us. Life! Death! Hunger! Sleep! The need for shelter, stress relief, and to connect with other beings. This epiphany began to glisten to me like the sun.

These are the types of things I was pondering during my sleepless nights. Another thing I came up with: Memories are like the big SUVs that constantly need refueling. The question is — What filling station are *you* pulling into? What are *you* filling them up with: Pride, Shame, Guilt, Embarrassment, Anger, and Suspicion? For all of us, those memories which are fueled by emotions seem to get the best mileage.

All in all, those days flew by quickly. I typically ate around 7:00 A.M. or when I felt hungry. After hanging around the house and doing odds and ends there, I looked to be gone by 10:00 A.M. and would return by midnight if possible. Sometimes my brother would go with me, and sometimes my wife would go, but no matter who went, I was going.

So far, at least, the vibes between my wife and I were still solid. Although, at one point, I had to convince her of the need to ask for more time from her job. I could tell she was supportive, but that some reluctance was still there where her job was concerned. Things worked out perfectly. She was able to take off for two weeks. She made arrangements to meet with the insurance adjuster to see what damage was covered by our homeowner's policy, and what could I do but accept her decisions? Also, when she asked me whether we should contact FEMA to see if we were eligible for any assistance, I had to admire her, because the thought hadn't even crossed my mind. She took me through a whole checklist of things on her to-do list, and I had nothing but respect for everything she was doing.

In truth, what Janet was saying was hitting me like musical stabs. They were a pleasant surprise. And for a moment, I was tempted to make a 360-degree turn from the direction I had taken and start spending more time at home. I thought about that for a split-second, but eventually I had to shake my head at that, because as uncharacteristic as my absence appeared, I knew deep down I was doing God's Work.

PRIVATE PAIN

God was erasing me and redrawing me continually. Naturally, I didn't want to burn bridges, but sometimes the only thing to do was to get practical by jumping into the fray of the work which needed to be done by rolling up your sleeves and getting in where you fit in.

But it is also, I imagine, a way to keep the fear and uncertainty of the situation at bay — and somehow make yourself feel like you have some control over a seemingly uncontrollable situation, especially the situation wrought by Katrina who came in and threw everything out of whack to the point of bringing us to our knees. And with me being a man of God, it was, "Do or die."

I never jumped and never will from the thin line of joy and pain. Needless to say, the situation was problematic. There was so much to do that I had problems keeping up. My load of responsibilities had increased, and I was going non-stop. I wasn't necessarily having fun, and I did find it increasingly difficult to give people the attention and consideration they deserved (with my wife being a case in point). I could only appease myself with the understanding that I was at least present. I was on the scene doing this work until my next Divine Assignment came.

I could tell that my wife was being polite by referring indirectly to my potential flameout by saying, "You need to slow down and take some time for yourself."

The thing is, despite the limited resources — including energy — I simply had to do more. I had to do what I had to do to help others get through this situation. I couldn't stop time to entertain the psychodynamics. Whether it was food for a hungry belly or a word of wisdom at the right time to help someone get through, there was no half-stepping for me. I know the evil that men can do, so it was time to show the other side of the coin.

Dr. DeBruce Nelson

My behavior wasn't just rash behavior. I felt my wife's pain, and I know others were suffering from me being pulled from all directions. And at times, my blood pressure was rising almost as quickly as the demands which were being made on me. And for that, a part of me knew that I would soon be experiencing the repercussions. The obligations seemed oppressive, but at the same time, this was an incredible opportunity to show the kindness that was missing in a world growing colder by the day, as we search for mansions, yachts, and caviar dreams.

Despite feeling harried and pressured, heroes of faith are made by one faith-deed at a time.

Thinking of that reminds me of the story of Miep Gies. I don't know how many people have read *The Diary of Anne Frank*, but whether you have or haven't, the lady who helped Anne and her family was a lady named Miep Gies who served as their lifeline to the outside world. The family up in the attic hiding from the Nazis couldn't run the risk of leaving, so they needed someone to serve as a go-between. So Miep, a 22-year-old pregnant Dutch woman, stepped up to meet the challenge. She was loyal, brave, and courageous in generally proving that she could raise above her own self-interests — putting others' safety before her own. Miep came to the Franks as much as possible, bearing news, food, clothes, and other necessities. Miep's willingness to risk her life to protect those illegal Jews from the Nazis who were intent upon killing them showed that sometimes you have to rise above the dire circumstances.

To me, Miep had the right frame of mind. The situation called for someone to rise up and meet the unprecedented challenges. If I wanted to make sure God has soldiers on the front line, then for me, there was no retreat and no surrender. Let's view this from a different angle. Being a country boy, I know that if you want to be proficient with horses, you have to ride bareback, which will teach you how to maintain your balance. Riding bareback will

PRIVATE PAIN

test you because you have no control over the horse's movements; you have to get the feel for it. At first, when you start riding bareback, you better go slow until you're sure that the horse can handle your weight and leg placement, and then once you both have a feel for each other, you can begin to trot. Also, when you ride a horse bareback, you can't look down at the horse, you have to focus on where you are trying to go. Lastly, you gotta learn to sink your heels deep and just ride.

That's why, to me, my going back to Biloxi was a matter of perspective, the lens you view the world from. To me, it was the time to encourage, influence, teach, and learn. It wasn't just about the nature of this catastrophe, but it was about my response to this natural catastrophe.

Sure, I wanted to provide for my family, but if my wife or anyone else could have really looked into me at this time, they would have seen that this was my life's mission. If I missed something at home, as far as I was concerned, it had to be *charged to the situation*. Otherwise, I wanted to show my family by example that God was going to take care of us for taking care of His people. I wouldn't waste my time telling you this if I didn't believe it. Yeah, I didn't have all the Xs and Os worked out, or, in other words, I didn't know how it was going to all come together; I just believed it could. The opportunity was here to put my beliefs into action.

> I thought about a quote I once heard. "Vision without actions is merely a dream. Action without vision merely passes the time. Vision with action can change the world."

Likewise, to take on the role of being the inspirational lynchpin is what I was called to do, but even this has its limits, and I know that. I realized that when the phone calls stopped. I made up my mind that no matter what, I was going to fight any negativity that sought to break my stride or that threatened to take away my testimony as a loyal soldier in God's Army.

I thought about a quote I once heard, "Vision without actions is merely a dream. Action without vision merely passes the time. Vision with action can change the world."

From that point on, I made a vow to get out of my own way the moment I became conscious of it. This was no easy feat, because as you try to keep functioning, the enemy is looking for access points. What God was showing me was that for all of the despair, you have to have an equal dose of grit and vision.

I didn't want to underestimate God's Grace, so I had to try and relax as He changed me for the better. I say this, but please, don't get me wrong; it was very difficult to give God fuller access to my system. I was trying to allow Him to work through me like the Old Testament Prophet Ezekiel. I felt as if God kept asking me, *"Son of man, can these bones live?"* Of course, I've got to be ready when he says, *"This is what the LORD Sovereign LORD says to these bones."* (Ezekiel 37.4)

Hope in a Hopeless Situation

Prophet Ezekiel's famous vision, The Valley of Dry Bones, was given to him more than 2500 years ago for the Babylonian exiles. However, God's question to Ezekiel, *"Can these dry bones live?"* was a question still addressed to me. At times, we ask it of our lives, our marriages, our crises, our nation, and our environment. This striking vision was a prediction and a promise from God that He would deliver Israel out of captivity and return them to their home. In my judgment, I saw everything tied and dried up like the dead bones. I felt Katrina had left us lifeless and that only God had the power to give us real life.

PRIVATE PAIN

While driving back to Biloxi, there was a mixture of anticipation and dread, but what can you do except pray that God gives you strength to endure. Each day, as I was in this battered place, I had to keep telling myself, *Be Not Afraid*. I knew that this could have been the effective end of my preaching assignment, unless I fought and unless I allowed God to direct my steps. Yet my composure was challenged with every situation that had cause for a miracle. But what can you do when one miracle simply just won't do?

Since I was not afraid to refrain from believing that God would meet lofty expectations, I was ready for whatever would come. Since things were getting rather complicated, I had to adjust my mind to receive the worst, believing that God could redeem *any* situation. And in one particular case, that meant saying goodbye. As they say, "Departing is such sweet sorrow." As it happened, many of the saints who I had come to know and love decided that their time in Biloxi had come and gone. When they told me this, there was a moment of awkward silence between us.

Yet I couldn't think like the average person. It was time to let these people go, especially when my spirit confirmed in me that this was the right thing to do, for this particular set of people, and at this particular time.

Sadly enough, some had left before Katrina and had simply never returned. Others decided afterward that it was time to go. So, that meant me saying goodbye to a large part of me. I did with one particular family — and watching them drive off, I was determined to let the positive reign over the negative, even though for a split-second I felt jaded. After all, these were people who you knew every nook of their hearty laugh and every cranny of their joy. I could see as they left that I was going to have to go to war with new soldiers.

Believe it or not, I understood why people left. After all, one of the hardest emotional aspects to this Katrina mess was not being able to talk with loved ones. This situation was scattering people all over, and because the communications were still down, many hadn't been able to put their minds or their friends' and loved ones' minds at ease. Unfortunately, this is how it went.

It's bad enough that you could see children crying because their parents were crying — and you knew these kids didn't understand the full weight of the tragedy. Sometimes, these scenes were like a wrecking ball coming against your positive mind frame. That's when you realized that it hurts; it simply hurts. This situation needed a special kind of healing. Thankfully, however, I wasn't the only person in this place still teetering on an emotional tightrope because of the initial horror and lasting devastation. One of the effects was that of displacement. To be brutally honest, it's really hard to convey, let alone understand, this type of displacement of people being shipped all over America, maybe forever, due to Katrina being a home wrecker.

It made me think about the situations which had occurred right after the Tsunami — that massive flood which left thousands of kids suddenly without parents, opening up the floodgates for foreign adoption. The situation had gotten so dire, so tight, that many had no choice but to displace those kids in the hope of a better life.

After saying goodbye to some of the saints, I was ready for change from moment to moment. A short time later, someone asked me to pray for an ailing relative. At first, I got weak-kneed at the prospect that God was testing me. As I went to find out, one way or the other, I silently prayed to God, *Father, please, these people ain't gonna believe in you unless you start showing them something.* I had to get off of that and change my mission to being a pure vessel.

When I got there, I laid my hands on the old mother and declared that God was the Healer that I knew He was. Upon leaving that scene, the relative called out to me, "Bishop, she gon' live, ain't she?"

Again, I wish there was a step-by-step manual for a crisis, but there isn't. What it came down to for me was — practice what you preach — live out your faith. With that in mind, I said, "You'll see; God gonna get the glory out of this."

They hugged me because they believed that I believed in what I was saying. *Whew, have mercy!*

I walked out there groaning to God, *You gotta come through, Big Papa.*

I hated to have misgivings, so every time a doubtful thought came, I shook it off while trying to be brave in the face of defeat. While walking the beat, people waved at me, and I waved back with full enthusiasm. As I did this, probably from my deep-seated anguish, something kept asking, *Who are you really, and what were you before?* God kept whispering to me, "*All things work for My good; all things work for My good*". The more I realized it, the more I realized that I had to admit to myself that I hadn't gotten on the wrong track to religion instead of the right track to Christ, so I shouted with fervor, "We're gonna make it back, even better than before!"

Of course, some wanted to debate about: "When and how?" and, "Later on or right now?" In fact, one saint came to me and asked me whether he should stay or go. As strange as it sounds, it came to me that the Holy Spirit is always on a mission; although, the Father and Son are united in Heaven, the Holy Spirit is always out and about, everywhere. On this particular occasion, I felt something which compelled me to tell the young man that God wanted him to stay in Biloxi.

"God wants you stay here and make a difference."

"Are you sure?" he asked, as if I had told him something he didn't want to hear.

I nodded in the affirmative, "As sure as God is my witness!"

He looked up to Heaven with a "Love me or leave me alone" glance, before staring at me with a dead-serious face, "I trust you; I'm gonna stay."

We hugged, and then I sent him off with words of encouragement, "Keep the Faith!"

This is how it was; in this spiritual storm... many were turned away; some were washed away, but either way, you have to realize that behind every storm, there are still pieces to work with.

You see, while making my rounds, whether on foot or in my truck, I saw so many things taking shape, because in these hours of desperation attitudes were forming, some for the worse, some for the better. There were more and more volunteers coming in, and the National Guard had set up checkpoints. It seemed as though the thoughts during this first week turned to search and rescue, then to food and water, and then to sanitation. As a result, the Biloxi City employees (Police, Fire, etc.) were on the scene working tirelessly to meet the stiff challenges that Katrina presented, with many neglecting their families and personal property to focus on the safety and welfare of the citizens of Biloxi. They set up points of distribution in each of these Biloxi locations: Cedar-Popp's Shopping Center on Cedar Lake and Popp's Ferry Roads, just south of the I-10 Cedar Lake exit, Wal-Mart at Pass Road in West Biloxi, Food Tiger Supermarket on Division Street at I-110 overpass, Chevron Station, Wool Market Road, and the Biloxi Community Center.

I was determined to make sure that I picked up what I could to provide relief. I had to make the people realize that God sees how much their pain hurts. After seeing the National Guard checkpoints set up on Division Street, I began to wonder if this was an overreaction to the looting. Then I realized that perhaps it was for President George Bush, because there was a buzz going around Biloxi that George Bush was coming on Friday. The thoughts of Mr. Bush coming conjured up images of that dumbfound look he had when he was told about the 9/11 terrorist attack while talking to those school kids. Then something prompted me to take a wait-and-see approach. For even deeper reasons, I knew that it was not time to rely on the Federal Government. It was about relying on God and each other. It wasn't about leaving it all now, leaving all the hard work to crash and fall down just because George Bush was coming. I didn't want to be 'Mr. Eyes Wide Open and Blind'. Still, with all of this George Bush hysteria, some people were overjoyed, while others were overly angry.

I had to pull one lady's face level with mine, and with my hand gently on her chin, I looked her in the eyes, "You are a child of the Most High God, not George Bush or any politician — Let God make a way for you, not them." The reason why I was saying this was because I knew most politicians make promises which they never fulfill, but God is faithful when He promises.

She looked me back in the eye, "You promise?"

"God promises you. Is that good enough?"

"Yeah, I'm sorry."

"It's okay; you're entitled to your feelings, but just filter them through God."

Repeatedly, I tried to reverse the fortunes of many of the beleaguered who were living in heartbreak hotel at the prospect of George Bush coming to neglect them. I did my best to redirect them, but some didn't want to be turned around from that position. Nevertheless, our crew had to keep spirits uplifted because donations were coming in from all directions. And, as we found out trying to minister to some of the people receiving donations, recovery was a matter of patience in some cases, even though time wasn't keen on waiting on any of us. That's funny, in an ironic kind of way.

Tragicomedy

"The balance is felt in the crying laughter of knowing and experiencing the comedy of the tragedy. To express its wholeness one must receive what you give...." — Rasa

A tragicomedy is a drama combining elements of tragedy and comedy. At times, this Katrina situation was full of tragicomedy because odd occurrences were happening continually. That's why I kept telling myself, *Expect to change and adapt. Every day, something changes.*

For instance, some people barely survived Katrina, but upon their return home, their wall clock was still ticking. Some people survived by floating on refrigerators, and then they couldn't get anything to eat for 24-48 hours. Some people lost prized furniture to the storm, but their unwanted furniture remained. Some who couldn't afford new cars found new cars in their driveways after Katrina; of course, they had been delivered by the storm. One casino was sitting on top of the Holiday Inn. There was a perfectly undamaged house, habitable except for the fact that it was upside down in the middle of a highway. The floodwaters had left grass up above our heads on the exterior walls of the house; videotapes and an ATM card were found in the walls. And there was a baseball game, or at least a baseball game sign, or maybe it was a soccer sign: *Katrina 1, Biloxi 0: Game Not Over.*

> **Some people barely survived Katrina, but upon their return home, their wall clock was still ticking.**

To add to the tragicomedy, the problem in those early days was the fact that many were finding out that on all levels, there was a lot of confusion and a lack of coordination. There were more help-wanted signs for roofing contractors and mold experts than there were roofing contractors and mold experts. And if people weren't vulnerable enough, property owners were warned to beware of transient contractors who typically set up shop in the wake of disasters such as Hurricane Katrina just to take advantage of people. On top of all that, a dusk-to-dawn curfew had been implemented. It was almost laughable because there was still so much desperation. Still, there had to be order and patience.

To go along with the above, leaders were telling residents not to drink the tap water or flush any toilets due to heavy damage to the wastewater system. Besides that, they needed whatever water pressure there was to fight fires. The bathroom tip put out was: Place a plastic supermarket bag in the bowl of your commode, with the handles of the bag overhanging the rim of the bowl. After use, tie the handles of the bag and drop it into your blue BFI trash receptacle. Or dig a ditch, which more than a few did — I kid you not. They say the best things in life are free!

Strategic Alliances

To get it all in perspective, despite all of this confusion and heartache, I saw this as a time for the 'Church Without Walls' to step up. With that said, I was thankful that Rev. Lee Bruner decided to come into fellowship with me so that we could run a 24-hour relief center. As such, Samaritans dropped off boxes full of bottled water, canned food, diapers, baby formula, or whatever they had to give.

Since we had put out the word that we were colorblind, many people from all walks of life came by to pick up supplies. But we didn't leave it at that; we let them know that God loved them and that He promise not to leave them or forsake them. When I sensed that a person had one foot in and one foot out of the church before this incident, I encouraged them to get right with Him. I mean that I encouraged them to be like Dorothy and use Katrina to find their way back home to where they belonged. I refused to allow them to stay down in the dumps without encouraging them to look on the brighter side of life. To me, the future had to be brighter than the present.

When a reporter asked me about how I saw the future, I proclaimed, "Within six months, the place would start coming back. Jobs will reappear and houses would be rebuilt. Lives would resume."

Rev. Lee took a different view, "A lot of things have to happen down here," he said. "People are living in houses where the roofs are torn up, the doors are blown off, and they have nowhere else to go. They're releasing people from the shelters with no jobs and no housing. And the insurance companies are telling people that since there was a flood along with the wind, and they don't cover floods, there is only so much they will pay. Isn't there something the Federal Government can do? Where are they?"

I respect Brother Lee's opinion, but this thing was as much about an internal response as much as it was about an external response. It is all God's property, even the human heart. He gave all of us free will, not to handcuff us, but because He loves us. Yeah, the government on all levels was missing the mark, but that didn't absolve every individual from keeping the faith. As crude as it sounds, you don't die with the government. You might die because of them, but you don't die with them. This was an individual thing before it ever was corporate — and make no mistake about that.

Now, despite me taking this view, it would get challenged, because someone might come to me wearing a distressed look.

PRIVATE PAIN

I could tell by the way they were choking back sobs that the situation was grave. Speechless, they summoned me by waving me to follow them. I followed them to one of the makeshift tents. Since Katrina was showing me by gauging my physical and spiritual senses as to what to watch out for, I could tell by the stench that death had showed up before me.

Man, I tell you, life ain't a dress rehearsal. When you see a mother dead in a tent — your natural man with all of his fear attributes messes with you. Stunned to the point of speechlessness, I felt like crying for the sheer hopelessness of it all. But when you see through the eyes of faith that death is not final — your spirit starts to rise up. Despite the fact that the natural realm has it in the submission hold; your spirit starts to stand up. That's when I realized that I had to give yet another bill to God.

> **But when you see through the eyes of faith that death is not final – your spirit starts to rise up.**

Yes, in the natural realm, this person died in a sad way, but on the flipside — the big *"But"* of God's Word was that this person had gone on to be with The Lord. It doesn't take away the emotional sting of death, but it does take away the darkness of the situation, inasmuch as it allows the light of truth to diffuse the situation. And freedom comes in knowing the truth. Nothing happens by accident. With that, I made my way over to the authorities and reported it.

After that incident, it was back to the grind. The sting was still there; don't get me wrong, but I realized that His Grace was more than sufficient for me. In saying that, I never really watched Soap Operas while growing up. Let me correct that, I would catch what they called "Stories" every now and then, but I never saw them as anything more than distractions or excursions from reality. I now see why people watch them. Let's leave it at that. Perhaps in an attempt just to provide myself with a sense of wellbeing, I wanted to put out the word into the atmosphere that God was going to emerge from this bad advertising. I wanted to tell the Devil so badly that his days were over fronting evil.

Pleeeeeze, I could hear something in me say.

There was no use arguing with myself, even though my soul let off a primal scream.

I had to be honest with myself. When I first decided to follow Christ, I knew what I signed up for. When you follow Christ, you are called into Divine Service, no ifs, ands, buts, or maybes about it — whether you accept the Divine Assignment or not. *God is always on our side, and he can turn any situation around. The questions are, "How?" and, "When?"*

The reality that time and chance happens to everyone (Eccl 9:11), became all too real to me at this moment. I might not like the way Katrina had walked through here and brought this ruckus with her, but she didn't have to steal the whole show. Yeah, she brought with her a spiritual storm which battered and shook people to the point of shaking some out of their faith, but there is joy on the other side of sorrow.

Katrina, war, mass murder, or any other potentially life-altering delivery system, forces you to look for answers. I came to understand that the voices you listen to during this time as a "faith" person makes all the difference. The problem is that we absorb so many different voices in our lives. We have to sift through the noise to detect the homing signal. It was no easy feat discerning between the other people's opinions, the enemy whispering in my ear, and the Voice of God.

Also, I began to understand that during these times you need to have solid faith in the people around you, and you have to watch out for the *hypocrites and the vampires*. You have to watch out for people who are more comfortable with speaking about Godly things than actually being about Godly things. You have to watch out for people simply focusing on the negative or people who want to suck the life out of a situation without offering any viable alternatives. Simply going back to the way things used to be won't cut it anymore in today's progressive world. I won't pretend that the cycles in life don't turn people cold, but as long as there is a God in Heaven who says that He can turn any situation around, that alone can be something to warm the heart.

Because of these types of dynamics, the magnitude of what you go through in a situation such as Katrina can make you tremble with both fear and excitement at the same time. Because of this, listening to the wrong person can tip you to the wrong side at the wrong time. Because, as sad as it is, we are often stuck between hope and tragedy, but the trick is, we have to learn to be content — no matter what. Again, the problem is in trying to uphold that public face we wear — the same brave face that shows you're holding up, while inside you are battered and bruised.

Pain Unspeakable

As if the DJ was playing the same song again, another death hit me just hours later. I knew then and there that I could just walk away, but something inside me was compelling me to carry on. Although I was crying everyone's tears, I couldn't show it; I had to show strength and stability. Even though my soul was shouting, *My God! My God! Why hast Thou forsaken me?*

I'll be honest; while 'Grief' was shadowboxing with me, for about an hour, I was tempted to quit every five minutes. I was tempted until I realized that some die with a name, and that some die nameless, but either way — death is inevitable. Snapped back to reality, that's when it hit me: Time is not stopping for death. I decided that from then on, I had to adapt a counter-puncher's mentality. I had to work my shots gradually until I got a clear opening.

Now, even though I felt pain which was unspeakable, what could I do — beyond praying? It's hard to describe exactly how I felt. Feelings can be complicated during rough times to the point that they become unexplainable, but God knows. Sometimes you feel like a broken man, but just like riding on 'Empty', you push it to the next destination and reevaluate your fuel situation then and there.

In the breakage — that fallen state — I was forced to give my life a fuller consideration. I was forced to search my heart and probe my mind, because these are soul components that impact the will. Now, ultimately, I had to ask myself if I wanted a full recovery. And after deciding that I did, I realized that I had to gain strength, a healthy perspective, an empowering viewpoint, and a positive outlook — if I wanted to healthily reconstruct myself. In fact, this second death put me in the exact position I needed to be in to *ultimately* make a decision one way or another. Again, sometimes it's better when you have limited choices — do or die choices. *You ain't gotta like it, but you gotta lump it.*

The Comeback

This situation of quitting got me to thinking about procrastination. The effects of procrastination can devastate anything from professional growth to your own personal relationships. As Shakespeare once put it, procrastination being "the thief of time" is all too familiar to us.

PRIVATE PAIN

Despite knowing the consequences, we've all done it; at one time or another we have procrastinated or put off something we know we ought to be doing. In this way, it's like a credit card; it's a lot of fun until you get the bill for it.

I suppose one reason we procrastinate is because we fear the results. We justify why we keep putting off the task at hand. Part of it is that we fear coming up empty-handed. Sometimes we are afraid of both failure and success. That's why sometimes it's better when success is the only option, because no matter what, we have got to give it a shot, because despite the frustration, it might be a once-in-a-lifetime opportunity to make a true difference.

Since I was closing the gap between what I preached and what I practiced, I refused to be brought down by the weight of expectations. I was not about to blow my top or flip my wig, instead, I was determined to see it through. Even though I recognized that the constant pain behind my eyes was an indication that I was dead tired and that my body was screaming for sleep, I wasn't about to put off the work that needed to be done. I couldn't let it all get away from me. Not at this time, even if I needed a confidence boost. True indeed, it would have to come as I went through doing what had to be done. Even if I occasionally stumbled into quicksand and was forced to listen to the Devil yakking over my head, telling me to stay in a "Sucker's Place", I wasn't going to allow my soul to phone in my resignation: "I quit."

Thomas De Quincy, an English writer from the 1800s, once said, "If once a man indulges himself in murder, very soon he comes to think little of robbing. And from robbing he comes to drinking and Sabbath-breaking and from that to incivility and procrastination."

In other words, watch those slippery slopes, because they go up as well as down.

Dr. DeBruce Nelson

In an odd way, as I was standing there thinking that I needed a doctor, here came one. He looked at me as if he knew I was overly stressed. Yet when he checked my vitals, I was normal. He told me that he knew God was keeping me, because given these conditions, I should have been ten times worse than I actually was. I thanked him, and I thanked God at the same time. Refreshed by that, I thought about dreams and obstacles.

In John Steinbeck's *Of Mice and Men,* the theme of dreams is explored through many characters in the novel. Steinbeck's point is clear; dreams have many obstacles. Dreams are hard to pursue. Dreams are a good ambition for people to have, but sometimes people run into obstacles along the way. Dreams are fragile, and obstacles often get in the way to fulfilling those dreams. The two leading characters in the novel, George and Lennie, both face obstacles to their shared dream of one day owning a farm and tending the rabbits.

The first obstacle that prevented Lennie and George from attaining their dream was that the law was after them. They couldn't attain their dream because they couldn't settle down long enough. Another obstacle was Lennie being mentally handicapped. That, coupled with him being a large man who acted child-like, made it a hard road to hoe for George and Lennie, which severely decreased their chances of making their dream come true.

The point for me is not that dreams are possible or impossible, but that they have obstacles embedded in them. Everyone has dreams, and all dreams have obstacles. Some dreams have obstacles that you can work through rather easily, and the seemingly impossible ones require you to dig as deeply as you can to overcome them.

That's why I had to be honest with myself, *What's my mindset, if it ain't a believer's mindset?*

PRIVATE PAIN

From what I saw in this catastrophe, some people just wanted to be touched. They were grateful just to know that you've taken the time to deal with them — that alone is a form of stress relief.

Also, this experience was showing me the value of working through the pain. You have to work through the pain in order to widen the lens from which you view God working in your life. Viewing God through the lens of punishment may prevent you from seeing the bigger picture. If you want to look through the Bible with a faultfinding lens and check off whenever you see something so-called negative about God, I am sure there is enough biblical evidence for it. But if you step back from that narrow human focus, you may be able to realize that God has a purpose beyond what we see or don't see. Instead of viewing events, like Noah's flood, from the destruction aspect, how about viewing it from the flipside so you can see that God gave mankind another chance. How you view God will determine a lot about how you receive *from* Him. A prime example of this comes from Scripture.

Think about this: Peter gave up everything to follow God — his fishing nets, his relationships, and the plans for his own life. He rose to the challenge when called and put himself under the direction and leadership of Jesus, wherever Jesus was taking him. To the point, Jesus, in Matthew 16:18, makes the famous "Rock" declaration toward Peter that is preached a million and four times each and every Sunday:

> *"From that time forth began Jesus to shew unto his disciples, how that he must go unto Jerusalem, and suffer many things of the elders and chief priests and scribes, and be killed, and be raised again the third day. Then Peter took him, and began to rebuke him, saying, Be it far from thee, Lord: this shall not be unto thee. But he turned, and said unto Peter, Get thee behind me, Satan: thou art an offence unto me: for thou savourest not the things that be of God, but those that be of men." (Matthew 16:21-24)*

Remember, God's Ways are higher than our ways; His Thoughts are higher than our thoughts. It was clear that Peter's thinking was out of position; it didn't line up with Jesus. Peter was looking at it from a limited, human viewpoint. Jesus was looking at it from a divine viewpoint. Peter's reaction is ours; we want God to line up with us, instead of vice-versa.

Too often we confront each other, instead of engaging each other.

After Jesus verified to Peter that he was indeed the Messiah and that he was going to be killed, this contradicted with Peter's human reasoning. Peter refused to accept this and wasn't going to let it happen. But Jesus, in setting him straight, let him know, *"Get thee behind me, Satan: thou art an offence unto me: for thou savourest not the things that be of God, but those that be of men."*

Now Peter, upon having a shock to his system, had a divine challenge placed upon him. He now had to put his human reasoning and fleshly desire in the back seat and trust God.

It doesn't matter, because in the following verse, *Then said Jesus unto his disciples, if any man will come after me, let him deny himself, and take up his cross, and follow me.* (Matthews 16:25)

Yet another limitless resource comes to us — unconditional love. In times like these, we are given faith and hope and love! During that moment, we rediscover that the greatest strength of all is love. It is love which empowers us to go on living into the future by making the most of the present moment. From what God was showing me, if you're grounded in love and the wind blows ferociously, your soul will remain anchored.

Chapter Five
TREASURE IN THE TRAGEDY

In a famous study by Victor and Mildred Goertzel, entitled, "Cradles of Eminence", the home backgrounds of 300 highly successful people were investigated. These 300 subjects had made it to the top. They were men and women whose names everyone would recognize as being brilliant in their fields, such as Franklin D. Roosevelt, Helen Keller, Winston Churchill, Albert Schweitzer, Clara Barton, Gandhi, Einstein, and Freud. The intensive investigation into their early home lives yielded some surprising findings: Three-fourths of the children were troubled either by poverty, by a broken home, or by having rejecting, over possessive, or dominating parents. In fact, 74 of 85 writers of fiction or drama and 16 of the 20 poets came from homes where, as children, they saw tense psychological drama being played out by their parents. Physical handicaps, such as blindness, deafness, or crippled limbs characterized over one-fourth of the sample.

How did these people go on, then, to such outstanding accomplishments? Happiness does not come from the elimination of pain, but from the realization of your purpose. When you make a deliberate decision not to give up, then life seems to present opportunities you hadn't thought of or couldn't have created yourself.

When *"Acts of God"* come, as they call natural disasters, we see how indiscriminate they can be as they wreak havoc, turning things inside and out. You see the best and the worst; the best in the worst of us, and the worst in the best of us. Disasters caused by nature, accident, or illness can bring immeasurable trauma, and at the same time, they can inspire the living to act in heroic and sacrificial ways. Hurricanes are thought and considered as something mankind could do without. But, recently, I learned that they are necessary to maintain a balance in nature. These tropical storms, with winds up to 150 miles an hour and accompanied by torrential rains, glaring lightning, and rumbling thunder, can be devastating. Yet scientists tell us they are tremendously valuable. They dissipate a large percentage of the oppressive heat which builds up at the equator, and they are indirectly responsible for much of the rainfall in North and South America. Meteorologists, therefore, no longer use cloud-seeding techniques to prevent them from being formed. They are convinced that hurricanes actually do more good than harm.

The Bible teaches us that the afflictions of God's people are like that. Though they bring temporary pain and grief, they can produce eternal dividends. (Psalm 119:75)

During my adult life, I have come to believe that people are more important than things. When one is younger, one is more driven to think that things are the route to happiness. Materialism is still as seductive as ever. To a great degree, materialism is the major driving force of our society. We live in a consumer society, and everything seems to be geared to that end. I am not against having things, but anyone who has had any experience with things can tell you that things, while nice, do not ultimately satisfy the deepest longings of the human heart.

Things are temporary; people are eternal, and God created us to be in relationships with people. When those relationships are healthy and positive, they can be extremely fulfilling. On the other hand, when those relationships are unhealthy and negative, they can be extremely discouraging.

All of us want positive relationships with others. Most of us have experienced the joy which comes from significant people who have made a positive contribution to our lives. And deep-down inside, we want to be that kind of person for someone else. We want to make a difference to someone else. We want to be a blessing. When people see us coming, we want them to be glad. So, how does this happen? How can we become a blessing?

Being A Blessing When I Needed A Blessing

How can I be someone's blessing when I am in need of so many blessings myself? The World has become a selfish place, where blessings are seldom counted. We go about our busy, introverted, and material lives with scarce regard for our fellow human beings. And whilst we loose sight of love, kindness, and compassion, we also deprive ourselves of the joy which only comes from blessing others.

> *"It is right for me to feel this way about all of you, since I have you in my heart; for whether I am in chains or defending and confirming the gospel, all of you share in God's grace with me. God can testify how I long for all of you with the affection of Christ Jesus. And this is my prayer: that your love may abound more and more in knowledge and depth of insight, so that you may be able to discern what is best and may be pure and blameless until the day of Christ, filled with the fruit of righteousness that comes through Jesus Christ—to the glory and praise of God." (Philippians 1:7-11 NIV)*

Paul feels justified in being thankful for the Philippians. He stood to them in the relation of father to children in the gospel; how could he, then, do other than rejoice in the evidence they gave, after all those years, that they were indeed *"partakers of grace"*? It is plain that he loved them and that they loved him. In Christ, we are all brought together in love. That we can love one another is evidence that we belong to Christ. Love is a work of God in our hearts. Jesus said that our love for one another would be an evidence of our relationship with Him. In John 13:34-35, we read: *"A new command I give you: Love one another. As I have loved you, so you must love one another. By this, all men will know that you are my disciples, if you love one another."* Our love is evidence of our discipleship.

You can show love for others by what you do — in deeds. *1 John 3:18 (NCV), My children, we should love people not only with words and talk, but by our actions and true caring.* This great Apostle not only expressed his love to those for whom he cared, he prayed for them. If we want to be a blessing to other people; if we want to make a difference in their lives, then we must pray for them. Prayer makes a difference. Do you want to be a blessing? Do you want to make a difference in the life of someone else? Begin by showing love. Show it by what you say. Show it by what you do, and then pray for others. Pray earnestly. Pray faithfully. Pray daily. Pray that they may grow in love. We are all born to be a power of blessing to others. If you need something good to happen for you, do something good for someone else. It does not have to be anything big; it can be as simple as holding the door open for someone behind you — it does not matter whether you like the person or not, or even if you know the person.

When you get up in the morning, try thinking about what you can do for someone else, rather than what someone else can do for you. If you find the dishes in the sink from the previous night, just think how appreciative your significant other will be if the dishwasher is emptied and the dirty dishes are put in the dishwasher. Some people have the financial means to bless people, while others have to let their actions be their blessing to people. When you are doing good things for other people, good things will happen to you. You might ask, "When and what?" The only answer I have is, "You can't out-give God, and His Timing is perfect.

We all learned about the math reciprocal in school, and some of us paid more attention to it than others. But the Bible teaches us a lot about the reciprocal. So whether it was visiting people, receiving and distributing donations, helping to prepare meals, encouraging people, praying for people, arranging for homes to be de-molded, or standing the gap in whatever endeavor I partook, I may have felt like Hell on Earth at times, but each smile or "Thank you" brought down a little Heaven. It helped sweeten up the foul taste in my mouth.

I was strengthened, as I kept seeing the number of volunteers steadily increasing in the devastated area. I felt the Holy Spirit encouraging me to have Church. Even if my regular saints were mainly gone, it didn't mean that I couldn't hold Church. Even if the building was wrecked inside, it didn't mean we couldn't hold it outside.

I felt The Lord assuring me, as I kept telling myself, *If I set up, help will come.* I ran the idea by trusted members, and although the question of timing came up as a concern, I realized that, *The time is now!* By then it was Friday, and I struggled to hold onto the idea of holding Church on Sunday. So when I got home that evening, I ran the problem by my wife.

"We can do this, right?"

"If you are feeling it, then you might have to go for it," Janet answered. Her voice was tense, I thought, and anxious.

"Are you serious?" I asked. "I'll need you right there with me."

"You will?" Janet asked. She let out a long exhalation, "Oh Jesus, Bruce."

I put my arms around her. I squeezed her assuredly. She was still beautiful, and though the stress of the mess was visible, I knew she would be there in service.

I sat down and patted my knee, like always, when I wanted her to sit on my lap. But she refused and laughed about being too heavy. I pulled her down to sit anyway. She sighed and sat there for a minute.

Just sit here a minute more; you need to rest, too."

She rested her chin on my head and sighed some more.

I asked, "What's the matter?"

"Bruce, it's not out there."

"I know the service will be near the building, and I've got to fix it up really nice. We've got to do this for The Lord and the people."

"Well, if God told you to have service, then I'll be there."

"Service will start at 11:00, if anyone asks."

"Trust me. You'll see; God's gonna bless."

She tried to get up, but I held her tighter. Then she began to wrestle her way out of my arms. I've always had fun restraining her. That's something she doesn't like.

"Okay, okay, let me go or I won't be there."

"Oh, yes you will, too."

"There is something about this service that I know God's going to do something special in it."

"I'm on Division Street, right in the heart of the biggest mess. The one advantage is that we'll be the only church on Division Street having services. That's great coverage."

I put my arms around her and assured her that God was in control, "It's like I keep telling you, honey — Have faith in me."

Chapter Six
I THINK, THEREFORE I AM

King Solomon, who was the wisest man ever and the author of many proverbs, came up with the explanation for it all, *"For as he thinketh in his heart, so is he,"* Proverbs 23:7. Creative thoughts and innovative ideas rarely occur when we are sitting at our desks attempting to solve a problem; rather, they come to us in the unguarded moments when we least expect it. The question is, "Do we capture those ideas and act upon them? Or are they lost forever, never to be discussed or implemented?" Thoughts create harmony or chaos in every aspect of our lives. If you want to learn to soar above every situation in your life, you must learn to use your thoughts to create the reality of your choice.

The progressive development of man is vitally dependent upon invention. Had Alexander Graham Bell not thought that he could invent a device which would allow you to pick up a solid object with numerous holes in each end, one that you could hear from and talk into, as well as transmit your voice thousands of miles in lightning-fast time, you wouldn't have the convenience, or the ability, to pick up the telephone and talk to someone on the other side of the world.

If the Wright Brothers hadn't thought that they could create a machine which would allow people to seemingly defy the laws of gravity, then we wouldn't know what it was like, or be able to, board an airplane with the ability to travel from one side of the country to the other in a matter of just a few hours. Dr. Wayne Dyer writes, "All of our behavior results from the thoughts that preceded it... so the thing to work on is not your behavior but the thing that caused your behavior, your thoughts."

Dr. DeBruce Nelson

The crying humanity forced me to answer the call, and since the buildings were knocked down, I had to take it to the streets. I had to go to where the people were.

"I know that the black mold is growing and I can't live here anymore. This old Lighthouse bus has been a safe haven for me. It's the only place that has been safe to stay, but I refuse to leave my safe haven."

Saturday, September 3, 2005 was the 6th day after Hurricane Katrina. The night before, after sharing with my wife about having a church service in spite of the lack of electricity and rampant devastation, I went to bed but couldn't sleep. Judging from the progress so far, streets were being cleared and supply lines were being established — I was pretty confident that we could pull it off; however, I was getting a slight headache just thinking about it. Eventually, to keep the pendulum from swinging back and forth, I decided to go with my spirit and my gut instinct. When I *visualized*, I could see us holding service in the right lane of Division Street, just outside the church, and I saw us encourage people who were driving by or any of the new arriving volunteers to worship with us.

> **"All of our behavior results from the thoughts that preceded it... so the thing to work on is not your behavior but the thing that caused your behavior, your thoughts."**
> **Dr. Wayne Dyer**

The more I thought about it, the more my heart raced, but at the same time, I saw this as a great time to expose people to some of the Southern-style Black preaching that they probably had only seen on television. As far as I knew, it was only the Jehovah Witnesses and the Muslim camps where different people had come together

PRIVATE PAIN

to worship after the hurricane. But as far as I was concerned, these different types of people bled just like me, and there was no way I could stand the church not meeting after a crisis of this magnitude. In fact, due to Katrina, people from different races, lifestyles, and religions were working hand in hand. With that in mind, I realized that I could take this situation as an opportunity to put it in the atmosphere that God is bigger than any individual.

Katrina, and her whole sad chain of events, were getting better one step at a time.

Case in point: On that Saturday morning, things changed. I was standing there, handing out this and that, when a White volunteer from up North somewhere walked up to our distribution table.

"Hi there, I'm Patty," she said softly, while smiling.

"How you doing, Patty?" I asked, returning the smile.

"Mind if I help you guys?" she asked.

"Not at all," I replied, waving her on.

She came behind the table. There was silence. I could sense that there was a little apprehension on both of our sides, but I tried to convey through body language that she was more than welcome.

"So, what's your name?" Patty asked.

"My name is Bruce," I said.

"Hey, Bruce, I just came down yesterday to help or do what I can."

"Me too," I said with excitement, "Not coming down here yesterday, but doing what I can."

We both smiled.

"Is this your church?" she asked, pointing the building.

"Well," I said, "in that building is where we hold some worship services, but the church is in my heart."

"Mine too," she said.

We both smiled again.

After I introduced Patty to Janet and everyone else, we all distributed goods to whomsoever came. While talking, I invited her and her friends to come to church the following day.

When it was time for her to rendezvous with her people, I could see it in her eyes that she was touched by this faith interconnectedness.

"Well, see you tomorrow," Patty said with a smile.

"Yes, see you tomorrow," replied Paul.

This encounter was case in point that my life was changing every day in every possible way.

That afternoon and early evening, we scrambled to get the place in order. We were making provisions to hold service with and without power. As the evening came upon us, there was a strange orange/yellow sunset glow on the horizon. While discussing how beautiful this looked, someone plugged in an amplifier just to see if it would work, and behold — it worked! "Praise God! We've Got the Power!" We all hugged each other, and of course, we thanked God.

PRIVATE PAIN

We later heard from Power Company spokesman Kurt Brautigam that the power would be restored for all eligible customers by the end of the day, one week later, on Sunday, Sept. 11.

The fact that what began as a thought created a manifestation proving that thoughts have power. They have the power to create and the power to destroy. They can generate energy — or deplete it. Simply put, we are a product of our imaginations. The influence that our thoughts, ideas, perceptions, and interpretations have on our experiences and our minds have a direct bearing on reality.

"Finally, brothers, whatever is true, whatever is noble, whatever is right, whatever is pure, whatever is lovely, whatever is admirable--if anything is excellent or praiseworthy--think about such things." (Philippians 4:8)

The power of the mind can help us deal with the strife in our lives. Whatever thoughts we feed our mind — whether it be of fear, wealth, or of peace — our mind will manifest. The results we see are the direct results of the mind's response to the thoughts we feed it. Anyone who is going through hard times can focus their mind on their many blessings and start to feel grateful. It isn't that your life around you changes, in as much as your perception does. Some of my greatest lessons in gratitude have come from realizing what I have. I believe we should use our positive thoughts to find meaning in the existence we already have and to enrich our spiritual lives. Doubtless, positive thoughts and believing you are worthy of love and abundance will open you up to receive more of the same, but it is not some kind of magic spell, and it is not a secret.

James states that faith without action is dead. You do not just wish for a car; you earn money by working and saving. You have to work for your goals. Positive thinking can help you envision your success and make you open to new opportunities, but it won't pay your bills.

Dr. DeBruce Nelson

None of us consciously invites crisis into our lives. We do not look forward to the next life-threatening event to come our way. We have never received an invitation to celebrate a crisis in the life of one of our friends. The news of a crisis brings feelings of sadness, fear, and regret. No one wants to face death, financial ruin, loss of a job, or a divorce, nor do we wish these events on others.

After experiencing the devastation of Katrina, I was blessed to see another side of trauma. Out of the ashes of despair, I observed the power of love heal the wounds of a troubled family. I saw the news of death bring people together in a closeness which they had never dreamed possible. I watched as neighbors dropped racial barriers to help one another rebuild. I have seen parishioners reach down deep inside themselves to find a superhuman strength to overcome a physical disability. I saw despair turn people toward the power of God within them. I watched seemingly helpless people become spiritual giants, as they exercised the power of prayer to overcome an impossible situation.

Katrina brought out the inner strength we never knew existed. It was this which gave us daily direction. Crisis is an opportunity, not a certainty. You can choose to take advantage of the energy in a crisis, or you can surrender to the feelings of despair and hopelessness. The adventure begins when you choose to accept the challenge and use the circumstances in your life to grow. This painful and sometimes devastating situation is only a stepping stone to something far greater than you have ever imagined. Numerous people have accepted the challenges of life by transforming their ordinary lives in the face of crisis. Our choice to have church service became one of the greatest motivating factors amidst that crisis.

Chapter Seven
MIRACLE OR TRAGEDY, WE PRAISE GOD

On Sunday morning of September 4, 2005, we moved the church out onto Division Street. We placed a 20-foot carpet just outside. We then put thirty folding chairs out there, hoping more people would show up.

We began the service by striking up some old-time Gospel Music. I'd say we had about sixteen people to start out with: Black, White, and in-between. Since we allowed them to come as they were, they were dressed from sharp suits, to jeans, to NFL jerseys, to whatever they had.

At around 11 o'clock, I launched into it, "Tell the Devil we're outside right now, but we're going in!"

They stood up and clapped wildly.

I started with the radical yet forever faithful Psalm 23. I asked them to repeat after me:

"My soul will be restored. Yea, though I walk through the valley of the shadow of death, I will fear no evil."

Then I asked of the congregation, "Say, Shadow of death."

"SHADOW OF DEATH!"

Women sang and said, "Amen!"

The Unsung Heroes

As people drove by, they slowed their cars and rolled down their windows. I wasn't afraid to jump in front of them to let them know that God was here. I pointed to one such car and waved them to join us. Not surprisingly, they were not expecting to be a part of the church service.

I went back to the pulpit to give acknowledgements. I grabbed Sister Carrie Jackson, and together we acknowledged before God and the public for helping her survive as she clung in a tree for her dear life. I also gave a shout-out to Brother Atlas Brown, the one who saved the drowning man and carried him to safety.

"God was good! He saved them all! He beat the Devil! We are still here!"

I acknowledged Sister Brenda Boykin, who had just found out the day before that her mother and brother were still alive.

PRIVATE PAIN

In the middle of this, a battered Mitsubishi truck stopped cold on Division Street. The driver, a White woman in a John Deere ball cap, and her 18-year-old daughter were both covered in mud, and the pickup was laden with all their possessions. The mother honked and yelled to the congregation, then she started to cry as she closed her eyes, "He is the beginning and the end!" she shouted, "Thank You, Jesus!"

I encouraged them to join in with the women of the church to sing and praise God.

A couple of sisters ran to the driver's side of the truck and offered to hug the woman. The lady stopped and the sister rubbed her back as she hugged the lady. They praised God together, before the woman and her daughter drove off.

"Somebody shout, I'm a survivor," I yelled, "Tell the Devil we're outside right now, but we're going in."

Praising God No Matter Your Condition

The difficulties of life often cloud our vision and keep us from praising God. Praise, according to the Scriptures, is an act of our will that flows out of an awe and reverence for our Creator. Praise gives glory to God and opens us up to a deeper union with Him. It turns our attention away from our problems and onto the Nature and Character of God Himself. As we focus our minds on God and proclaim His Goodness, we reflect His Glory back to Him. The results can fill you with peace and contentment and transform your outlook on life.

Praise to God is what we offer in acknowledgement of God's Excellent Being. You might think that praise is the same as saying *Thank You,* but there is a difference. Thanksgiving describes our attitude toward what God has done, while praise is offered for *who* God is. Psalm 18:3 says, *"I call to the LORD, who is worthy of praise..."*

All believers are commanded to praise God! In fact, Isaiah 43:21 explains that praise is one reason we were created, *"This people I have formed for Myself; they shall declare My praise."* Hebrews 13:15 confirms this, *"Through Jesus, therefore, let us continually offer to God a sacrifice of praise - the fruit of lips that confess his name."*

Praise originates in a heart full of love toward God. Deuteronomy 6:5 says, *"Love the LORD your God with all your heart and with all your soul and with all your strength."*

"You will guard him and keep him in perfect and constant peace whose mind [both its inclination and its character] is stayed on You, because he commits himself to You, leans on You, and hopes confidently in You." (Isaiah 26:3 — Amplified Bible)

We praise God because of *who* He is, and *what* He has done for us. We praise Him because He is great and powerful. *"For the Lord is great and greatly to be praised,"* (Psalm 96:4). *"Be exalted, O LORD, in Your own strength! We will sing and praise Your power,"* (Psalm 21:13). *"Therefore David blessed the LORD before all the congregation; and David said: 'Blessed are You, LORD God of Israel, our Father, forever and ever. Yours, O LORD, is the greatness, the power and the glory, the victory and the majesty; for all that is in heaven and in earth is Yours; Yours is the kingdom, O LORD, and You are exalted as head over all,"* (2 Chronicles 29:10,11). *"Now therefore, our God, we thank You and praise Your glorious name."* (1 Chronicles 29:13)

"All nations whom You have made shall come and worship before You, O Lord, and shall glorify Your name. For You are great, and do wondrous things; You alone are God. Teach me Your way, O LORD; I will walk in Your truth; Unite my heart to fear Your name. I will praise You, O Lord my God, with all my heart, and I will glorify Your name forevermore." (Psalm 86:9-12)

"I will extol You, my God, O King; and I will bless Your name forever and ever. Every day I will bless You, and I will praise Your name forever and ever. Great is the LORD, and greatly to be praised; and His greatness is unsearchable," (Psalm 145:1-3). *"All Your works shall praise You, O LORD, and Your saints shall bless You. They shall speak of the glory of Your kingdom, and talk of Your power, to make known to the sons of men His mighty acts, and the glorious majesty of His kingdom. Your kingdom is an everlasting kingdom, and Your dominion endures throughout all generations."* (Psalm 145:10-13)

We glorify God because He is righteous: *"And my tongue shall speak of Your righteousness and of Your praise all the day long,"* (Psalm 35:28). *"I will praise the LORD according to His righteousness, and will sing praise to the name of the LORD Most High."* (Psalm 7:17)

We glorify God because He is faithful and true: *"O LORD, You are my God. I will exalt You, I will praise Your name, for You have done wonderful things; Your counsels of old are faithfulness and truth."* (Isaiah 25:1)

We praise God because of His mercy: *"Praise the LORD, for His mercy endures forever,"* (2 Chronicles 20:21). *"Praise the Lord! Oh, give thanks to the LORD, for He is good! For His mercy endures forever,"* (Psalm 106:1).

> *"Make a joyful shout to the LORD, all you lands! Serve the LORD with gladness; come before His presence with singing. Know that the LORD, He is God; it is He who has made us, and not we ourselves; we are His people and the sheep of His pasture. Enter into His gates with thanksgiving, and into His courts with praise. Be thankful to Him, and bless His name. For the LORD is good; His mercy is everlasting, and His truth endures to all generations."* (Psalm 100:1-5)

> *"You are my God, and I will praise You; You are my God, I will exalt You. Oh, give thanks to the LORD, for He is good! For His mercy endures forever."* (Psalm 118:28, 29)

The spiritual environment is obviously changed when God is praised. Look what happened in the temple while the singers (Levites) worshiped God: *"The trumpeters and singers joined in unison, as with one voice, to give praise and thanks to the LORD. Accompanied by trumpets, cymbals and other instruments, they raised their voices in praise to the LORD and sang: 'He is good; his love endures forever.' Then the temple of the LORD was filled with a cloud, and the priests could not perform their service because of the cloud, for the glory of the LORD filled the temple of God,"* (2 Chronicles 5:13-14). God literally came in there! He indeed dwells in the midst of praise! What a privilege for us to feel His Holy Presence and be blessed by Him! *"Because your love is better than life, my lips will glorify you. I will praise you as long as I live, and in your name I will lift up my hands,"* (Psalm 63:3-4). So, regardless of the good, bad, and ugly in our lives, the first thing we should always do is praise our almighty God!

Hindrances to Praise

Praise is both important and powerful. So why is it so difficult at times to praise God? The Bible explains that, even with the power of the indwelling Jesus, our hearts are still *"more deceitful than all else,"* (Jeremiah. 17:9). We sometimes forget that we are always dependent on God to live victoriously in this life.

Satan, therefore, tries to persuade us that we will eventually reach a point where we can "Do it ourselves." The Scriptures are clear that Satan *"prowls about like a roaring lion, seeking someone to devour."* (1 Peter 5:8)

Disguised as an "Angel of Light", the Devil and his host will subtly seek to subvert the praises which the children of God owe to their Heavenly Father. God, however, has given us grace in times of need, provided we humble ourselves (Matt. 23:12; James 4:5-10). Praising God allows us to defeat the strategies of the enemy. As God's adopted children, we no longer have to remain slaves to sin (Gal. 4:6-7). We have a powerful spiritual weapon in praise, and it is guaranteed to be effective. (II Cor. 10:4-5)

Hearts of Gratitude

Because of the success of the outside service, we decided to hold a cookout for Labor Day (the following day). Why not? — That was our reasoning. There was a need for people to be connected, and we intended to satisfy that need. A group of volunteers and ladies from the church began cooking stews and chicken in 30-gallon vats for hungry residents. We did it because many people just wanted a hot meal.

I recently came across a description of our America in 1903. It stated that Only 14% of homes in the US had a bathtub. Only 8% had a telephone. A three minute call from Denver to New York cost $11 in an economy where the average worker made between $400 and $2000 a year. There were only 8,000 cars and 144 miles of paved road. The average life expectancy was 47 years of age, and 90% of all US physicians had no college education. The 5 leading causes of death were pneumonia, the flu, tuberculosis, diarrhea, and heart disease or stroke. Of all children, 95% were born at home. Most women washed their hair only once a month and used borax or egg yolks for shampoo. Marijuana, heroin, and morphine were all available over-the-counter. Crossword puzzles, canned beer, and iced tea hadn't been invented yet. There was no Mother's Day or Father's Day. Only 6% off all Americans had graduated from high school, and one in 10 adults couldn't read or write. (From "Planet Proctor" by Phil Proctor in *FunnyTimes*, November, 2003, p. 11)

Despite our problems, we are blessed to live in a pretty interesting era, with expanded opportunities for self-realization for a pretty wide spectrum of the population. Appreciate the world around you. Appreciation is a fundamental spiritual disposition that Christianity highlights and underscores. In Colossians 3:12-17, Paul the Apostle encourages us to cultivate a life of gratitude:

> "Therefore, as God's chosen people, holy and dearly loved, clothe yourselves with compassion, kindness, humility, gentleness and patience. Bear with each other and forgive whatever grievances you may have against one another. Forgive as The Lord forgave you. And over all these virtues put on love, which binds them all together in perfect unity. Let the peace of Christ rule in your hearts, since as members of one body you were called to peace. And be thankful. Let the word of Christ dwell in you richly as you teach and admonish one another with all wisdom, and as you sing psalms, hymns and spiritual songs with gratitude in your hearts to God. And whatever you do, whether in word or deed, do it all in the name of The Lord, Jesus, giving thanks to God the Father through him."

Chapter Eight
DISASTER RECOVERY PROCESS

After a disaster, recovery can take time. Staying connected to my family and friends during this period helped me to cope with the tragedy. It is not good to wait until something bad happens to realize that you love your parents, your spouse, your children, or your in-laws. I heard numerous stories from Hurricane Katrina victims who said, "It wasn't until this happened in my life that I realized how distant my family was . . . and how precious their lives are to me. I would give anything to backtrack time."

That is the way many feel when tragedy and sickness comes to a family. Don't wait until something bad happens to quietly look at the lives you are responsible for and the lives of those who need you.

Most people wait until disasters happen to examine their spiritual condition. Too often, people wait until they've lost their health, their marriage, their happiness and their peace of mind before surrendering to God. But you don't need to hit rock bottom before changing directions. Your life's trajectory can be altered significantly just by making simple adjustments to the way you think and act on a daily basis. God is in charge of everything in our lives! He plans everything in our lives and in our world. He is the same, yesterday, today, and tomorrow. The Lord doesn't want you to have a personal relationship with Him just so He will protect you from disaster or get you out of a crisis. Jesus died for our sins so that He could live in our hearts and bless us each and everyday!

Dr. DeBruce Nelson

One Month after Katrina

The weeks after Katrina were the most challenging of my adult life. Not only did it take me nearly two weeks to get more than six hours of sleep a night, I had to do it while dealing with one grief event after another. I had to deal with goodbyes, recoveries, and, of course, death. I didn't mention it before, but we found a whole family dead in their attic. Just thinking about it causes my skin to tingle and imaginary tap dancers to perform behind my eyes. The thing is, God helped me to eventually see that whatever I was seeing was a weigh station to pull into and get a better understanding of Him. It was showing me how to reintegrate the parts of myself that Katrina had split apart. In this way, I was like the scarecrow, as I was slowly coming into a fuller being.

I needed God to do this work in me, because I needed to be cool under fire. Because, after a month, East Biloxi, or "The Point", was starting to resemble a Third World country, insofar as stretches of it looked like shantytowns. There were still piles of debris everywhere, and many people were still sleeping in tents outside of their houses. In some ways, it looked like they were being punished, except in this case the punishment didn't fit the crime.

I hated to think that the drinking I started to see was directly linked to Katrina, but I am not that naïve. Essentially, what I started to see were people drinking from sunup to sundown to deal with their blues. This was unfortunate, because while some people shipped out to other parts of the country, others were allegedly told by FEMA that they had to wait by their homes to receive their FEMA trailers. This was a pressure-packed situation; then again, it was just another slice of the Katrina pie.

It is from this fact that I knew I had to change the nature of my relationship with myself and my Creator, and without turning back, because the devastation of Katrina puts you under pressure

PRIVATE PAIN

to lead by example — to match your walk with your talk. Due to this, the first part of my recovery was breaking through my self-absorption. That was a critical function, and the only way in which I saw that happening was to allow God to redirect my thoughts about what I was feeling about my life — and about society in general. I had to get below the surface to see things from a root standpoint and not just a fruit perspective. Also, I realized that as a minister of the Gospel, part of my Divine Assignment was to reflect on what's taking place in our society and to make sure I internalized it to find out what God had to say on the subject.

So, I began to think and reflect on a particular Christian theme, namely, the spiritual combat of the soul. As I saw it, this was a permanent fight. One in which you have to stay in a state of readiness, just in case a war broke out.

> **The crying humanity forced me to answer the call, and since the buildings were knocked down, I had to take it to the streets. I had to go to where the people were.**

Many times, when I started to reflect on deeper notions, something inside of me would say, *Puh-leeze!* I realized during these times that the old saying "Nothing to fear but fear itself" takes up residence in your soul. That's when your breath tries to run the hundred-meter dash, and you have to just *pause*. During that pause, that's when you flip the script, and instead of speaking from the negative, you make the connection with Romans 8.28, *"And we know that in all things God works for the good of those who love him, who have been called according to his purpose."*

Another striking thing for me was in understanding change, or drastic changes. With so many people who you've grown to love being uprooted, you begin to realize that this situation is not going to adapt to you, but that you must adapt to it. She is the baby that wants to be pacified or fed, despite you having a headache. You can't just put the baby in front of the TV and expect it to be quiet. You can't just shake it. You have to deal with it.

Another life-altering aspect which Katrina showed me is that *I don't have all the answers*. Katrina forced me into a part of ministry that was new to me. The crying humanity forced me to answer the call, and since many of the buildings were being gutted or knocked down, I had to take it to the streets. I had to go where the people were.

During this time, I began to make unique and wonderful connections which I might not have made if it weren't for Katrina. For instance, *I need to believe that something extraordinary is possible*. I connected with this thought, because in many ways Katrina had confronted me with my fears and phobias. There were so many different meanings in my head that frankly got realigned and were continuing to be realigned in Katrina's aftermath. Thank God, He showed me that to accomplish the extraordinary, I had to yield to the Holy Spirit and let Him lead the way.

As strange as it seems, I likened the Holy Spirit to a guide dog. Before you grimace at this, you must realize that guide dogs are great companions, confidants, and walking partners. Many a blind person depends on their guide dog every single day to help them navigate around people, obstacles, and situations. The person will adapt their lifestyle to this incredible helper, utilizing it to its fullest potential, and, in return, their confidence rises as they focus on the big picture, even though they are visually impaired or totally blind.

As I have illustrated, that part of what the spirit was illuminating to me was to change my approach in dealing with diversity. It was an effective tool in allowing me to expand my thinking base. After all, you don't have to be an Eagle Scout or the Employee of the Month to seek not your own. But to see past the circumstances of your own pain to minister life unto others requires you to be developed enough in your spirit to go to the heart of the matter.

At times, you feel like you can't afford to change back to Clark Kent. When thoughts like that creep up, you have to yield to the Holy Spirit. From nowhere, a voice inside of you will say, *It ain't about me.*

The more you do this, or at least the more I did it, my racing heart would slow down. I got dry mouth less and less. And my constant sweaty palms became drier and drier. In this way, the Holy Spirit becomes the variable. Realizing this made all the difference in the world to me. I realized that my response to this adversity was contingent upon how developed my spirit was and my receptiveness to allow Him to position me where He wanted me to be, and not just what was comfortable. How we respond will say a lot about our positioning within His Divine Plan. That's why spiritual perception requires wisdom, which has the ability to go past our senses. Like spiritual Love, it goes contrary to your senses, because 'Forgiveness' is higher-ordered thinking — out-of-this-world thinking. Again, I cannot stress enough how God was showing me not to limit Him by how I think my five senses work.

Building Back

I guess the old saying "Persistence Pays Off" may really be true after all, because we were able to start building back the church within two weeks. We were able to secure help from Compassion Central in the build-back process, and many

Dr. DeBruce Nelson

volunteers continued to come down to Biloxi to lend a hand. They battled with mosquitoes and had to sleep in tents to match how most of the community was living. Because of this, we were able to tackle the growing process of toxic mold. Mold work involves scraping the mold off of all the wooden surfaces in the already gutted-out houses, vacuuming all of the horizontal wooden surfaces in the house (floors, crossbeams, and rafters), and wiping the wood with a strong disinfectant to prevent new mold from growing.

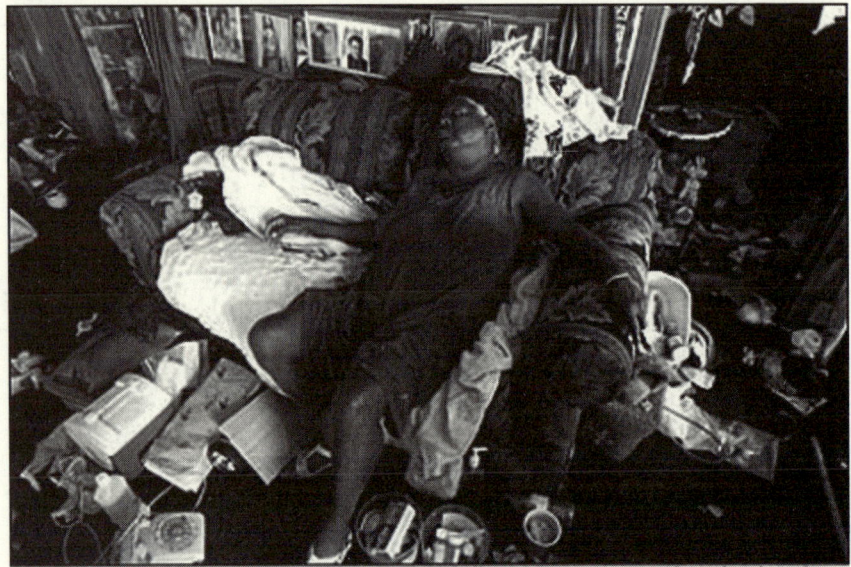
The Dallas Morning News / Michael Mulvey

An ailing Eddie Mae Smith collapses on her sofa in the living room of her mold-infested home in Biloxi, Miss. Local pastor Bishop DeBruce Nelson came to check on Smith, 75, and found mildew growing on everything. She had been living there since Katrina hit. — The Dallas Morning News reported.

PRIVATE PAIN

I had to check on Eddie Mae

Pastor DeBruce Nelson of Biloxi, Mississippi, (second from left above with his wife and relief volunteers) reveals a resilient spirit with these words, "Katrina broke our windows, but it didn't break our spirits."

Six Months After: From Private Pain To Public Praise

Six months later, there were still challenges. Many of the neighborhoods were still slow to come back. Although they were rebuilding casinos, the people were slow to matriculate back to Biloxi because there were no homes. Gone were the trucks and SUVs loaded down with food, water, and fuel that clogged the highways. Still, trees lay across broken houses, and piles of debris and garbage waited for pickup along the roadside.

It took FEMA five weeks to start delivering upon the promised trailers. Because of that, more and more people were still living in tents. Their homes were either still in shambles or in piles of debris where the bulldozers had rolled through. A few government trailers sat next to wrecked homes.

As of February 2006, the Federal Emergency Management Agency (FEMA) reported the distribution of over $286 million and 10,444 travel trailers in Harrison County. In March 2006, the City of Biloxi reported that over 2 million cubic yards of debris had been removed from city streets and rights-of-way at an estimated cost of $50 million and that sales tax revenues were down 19% in December 2005 from the year previous.

Rebuilding

When they announced that casinos were going up first, I was stunned for a moment. I never saw the enemy's house come up before the House of God.

After days of sitting in front of the church, looking down Division Street and wondering how will we be able to completely restore the House of God. One morning, I had picked up a copy of the *Sun Herald*, and I read that by December 2nd the first casino would open.

My goal was to have the sanctuary ready for worship before the casino opened, but I saw no way. Suddenly, a news reporter walked up and asked, "How are you, pastor?"

"Not so good," I answered. "I'm reading here that by December 2nd the first casino will open its doors." I asked the reporter, "Does your camera work?"

"Yes," she responded.

"Start rolling."

"I bring the enemy notice this day that before the casinos open their doors, there will be one church in East Biloxi with its doors open. If the Body of Christ is listening this morning or watching this film, help me raise the House Of God before the casinos open."

Two weeks before the casino deadline, Lighthouse opened her doors. Our God is a strong God. He is Awesome! The casinos opened on their proposed date. Everyday they delayed opening we gave God more glory!

My faith kicked in. It made me realize that there is a spiritual war going on that no man can afford to ignore. Songs like "What A Mighty God We Serve" became resident in my soul. Then it dawned on me; Satan snatches the word. He is the one who makes us tired when we are reading the word or trying to pray. He is the one who brings up the thousands of things we need to do instead of doing what we need to do. He joins with our natural flesh to misshape our priorities. And he knows that we have free will — he knows because God loved us so much that He had to give us free will to be free of the accusation of having created robots. He knows what it is like to think of yourself more highly than you ought to.

So, knowing that I'm in Divine Service, I decided that until I received my next assignment, I was going to walk in the orders of God. I was going to set the tone. I made up my crazy mind that I was going to change the atmosphere. I made up my mind to partnership with WHOMEVER to refurbish 100 houses.

Instead of letting the world set the tone, I let the Church set it, to tap into the measure of God in all of us.

Dr. DeBruce Nelson

The Devil's PR Department

The Bible has been so candied over the years that in the popular imagination, it has lost its creating-light-from-darkness launching pad. It's like how Jesus and Santa Claus are now, Siamese Twins. It's like a hologram image of Martin Luther King that when you turn it to one side, it becomes Gandhi.

That's why the Devil and public relations were made for each other. The Devil is constantly advertising to us one half of the equation. Too often advertising brings about all the wrong feelings when it is displayed on television. It shows how "Smirnoff Vodka" can make a person have a great time at a party, but what it does not tell you is that it can injure your liver, and if any person consumes too much, it can also kill them.

This type of ad has a subtle but negative effect on today's society. It suggests that drinking is fun and exciting, and then it makes a person think that it's okay for anyone to drink and have a good time. A Smirnoff bottle comes in many different flavors and colors, such as Green Apple, Orange Twist, etc. These cool-looking ads are persuasive because they emphasize fun at every turn. They focus on the positive and don't attempt to create balance. These ads appeal to that desire in us to have fun. They correspond to our emotions that want one-sided freedom. The ads speak to the pleasure principle. So when you see people having fun and drinking Smirnoff Ice, maybe it appeals to your appetite to have a good time, and so some want to have the same fun that the ads are showing. These things drive commerce and business; they desire to satisfy our physical needs.

I say all of this because Katrina showed me that the Devil has a 24-hour Public Relations Department responsible for protecting his image.

Christ's PR Department

On a deeply personal level, I will put this out there and you can take it or leave it. I tell you that the work which took me seven years to put right before took four months to put right after the storm. The House of God came back bigger and better than ever. Enough said!

People say the best things in life are the things which we are most scared of. Love is not a thought but a feeling which many say is eternal. Deep down, you'll always remember your loved ones. Most people take love for granted; they don't look after it and don't realize what it can do to you or someone else. These days, the term love is confused with sex.

Positive Outlook

We each inhabit two worlds — worlds that are often as far apart from each other as two worlds can be. One world is the revealed portion of our existence: our professional, social, and family lives, and our conscious thoughts and feelings. At the same time, we inhabit a hidden world, a world of subconscious drives and desires which have innately known truths and deeply held convictions which rarely, if ever, see the light of day. My understanding of this became the premise for writing this book.

The term "smoking gun" is a reference to an object or fact which serves as conclusive evidence of a crime or similar act. Its name comes from the idea of finding a smoking (very recently fired) gun on the person of a suspect wanted for shooting someone, which in that situation would be nearly unshakable proof of having committed the crime.

Dr. DeBruce Nelson

Often times, our own human nature serves as a counter-terrorist working for the enemy. It searches for the smoking gun in our lives. Their investigation is trying to zero in on our concealed weapons — our secret sins — and they would love to come out publicly with their findings. Sometimes, as long as we are content, there is no need to break/disrupt/alter our course. Simply by removing the hedge of protection or one of the buffers, we can easily fall out of our comfort zone.

Despite what I see going on, nothing can really do me harm, because it all works for the good. In my going out and coming in, I've learned to have a thankful mindset — to be a walking praise. Love looks forward; hate looks back, but fear looks all around.

It's hard to pinpoint the exact moment when it all came together, because it did not come back all at once. It is as it stands today, and it's coming back little by little.

Chapter Nine
TWO YEARS AFTER KATRINA

As I write this chapter, two years have passed since the onslaught of Hurricane Katrina, and East Biloxi is still gathering fragments of its past. Many of the residents have not returned. With the financial support of the Oprah Grant which East Biloxi received, we were able to rebuild some of the homes and restore some others. I have served as the Vice President of the East Biloxi Coordination Relief Development Agency. This grant money was a tremendous blessing in reestablishing normalcy to this area. Many of the residents are settled in brand-new homes.

A Cry of Help

There was a day when my pain was no longer bearable. I called the TV station and requested that they send a reporter over to film how fourteen people were living. These people were living in my old church bus that had gone under 18 ft. of water. The Lighthouse Church fed them daily. We had a frigid winter, and they had no heat — only their bundles, which included wool blankets that we issued them. Black mold was growing throughout the air-conditioning vent. The mold was growing by the minute. Several of the people were getting sick. Finally, it was too dangerous for them to continue to live on the bus.

The hardest task for me was to tell them that they had to leave the bus. There were women and men of different races living there. One of the most disturbing things which one of the men said as he was gathering his meager belongings was, "I know that the black mold is growing and that I can't live here anymore. This old Lighthouse bus has been a safe haven for me. It's the only place that has been safe to stay, but I refuse to leave my safe haven."

I didn't know what he was going to do. He gathered his blankets and left only to make his bed underneath the bus. That afternoon, the clouds darkened and the rains started. As I began to leave, I promised him that someway, somehow, I would help them. Shortly afterward, we did get help for them.

Weeks passed. I went over to Our Mother of Sorrows (church) for a meeting. This meeting was to solicit help for those people and for our Senior Citizens program, which was called "Senior 65/65" program. As I was leaving the meeting with a heavy heart and weariness, I heard a group of young men arguing. As I approached my car and had just gotten into it, one of the young men started shooting. Two of the fourteen rounds that were fired hit my car. One hit just below the passenger door, and the other shot hit my fog light. If the first bullet had been a bit higher, it would have hit me. It was in line with my seat. Praise God for Guardian Angels.

I asked myself, should I stay and confront them or should I speed away. Well, the wiser man won. I sped out of the way of them. That is when my spirit stood up in me and reminded me that no weapon formed against me shall be able to prosper (Isaiah 54:17). Of the 100 homes, 5 new homes have been completed, and house #27 is still in the refurbishing stage. With the extraordinary help of volunteers, many of the people are still praising God for their new homes. My plan was to ask a church to fund one house to completion. At this point, the entire vision is still not complete. Seems as though the funds are being held up. But I know that God is a provider, because He is our Jehovah-jireh.

Dr. DeBruce Nelson

ABOUT THE AUTHOR

The ministry of Dr. DeBruce Nelson has created tremendous impact for more than ten years on the Gulf Coast, bringing deliverance and salvation to hundreds. He is a 2003 graduate of Grace Seminary in Mobile, Alabama, a 2007 graduate of the True Holiness Bible Institute in Chesapeake, Virginia, a recipient of Leadership Award from Lighthouse Holiness Churches, Inc. Grand Bay, Alabama, a recipient of the World Vision Award, and a recipient of the NAACP award.

Dr. Nelson is a counselor and a founder of the House of Redeem and the 65/65

Senior Citizens Program. He pastors a mission outreach in Biloxi, Mississippi. Dr. Nelson serves as vice president of the Ministerial Alliance, the vice president of the East Biloxi Coordination of Relief and Redevelopment Agency. He serves as State Overseer of Mississippi, and he serves on the Board of Ministers under the leadership of his brother, Apostle Floyd E. Nelson, D. D.

Dr. Nelson has focused his recent efforts in spreading the liberated good news of the Gospel of Jesus Christ and on the replacement of many of the residents of East Biloxi. He also evangelizes across the South and parts of the North. He concentrates much of his ministry to those people who have no voice, the homeless, widows, and those who are socio-economically deprived.

Dr. Nelson's Men's Retreat, an effort to bring together ministers, pastors, deacons, and all laymen every other month, has been a huge success and a blessing to not only *his* ministry but to *theirs* as well. His objective is to encourage men to be men and to continue in the assignment with which God has given them.

Dr. DeBruce Nelson

Lighthouse Apostolic Holiness Church is located in Biloxi, Mississippi. Dr. Nelson is proud to be married to Janet Griffin-Nelson, and they have added to that blessed union one son, Rodney, and one daughter, Kaylan, and from them two grandsons, Andrew and David Griffin.

To contact Dr. Nelson, please write:
Dr. Bishop DeBruce Nelson
Lighthouse Apostolic Holiness Church
769 Division Street
Biloxi , Mississippi, 39530

Email: jgn719@centurytel.net

Please include your prayer requests and comments when you write.

Personal Notes

Personal Notes

Personal Notes

Personal Notes

ORDER FORM

Name _____

Company _____

Address _____

City _____ State _____ Zip _____

Telephone _____

Email _____

Please send me _____ copies of
"Private Pain, A Pastor's Struggle through Katrina"

Price	Shipping	Total
$15.95	$3.50	$19.45

Total Enclosed: $ _____

Books are available at special discounts for bulk purchases, sales promotions, fundraising, or educational purposes.

For more information about the author
or speaking engagements, write to:

Lighthouse Apostolic Holiness Church
769 Division St
Biloxi, MS 39530

Jgn719@centurytel.net

Or order online at: www.wpublishers.com

A portion of the proceeds will be used to help Katrina Survivors